EDI Retrospectives in Policymaking

Policymaking on the Front Lines

Memoirs of a Korean Practitioner, 1945–79

Chung-yum Kim

The World Bank
Washington, D. C.

Copyright © 1994
The International Bank for Reconstruction
and Development / THE WORLD BANK
1818 H Street, N.W.
Washington, D.C. 20433, U.S.A.

All rights reserved
Manufactured in the United States of America
First printing October 1994

The Economic Development Institute (EDI) was established by the World Bank in 1955 to train officials concerned with development planning, policymaking, investment analysis, and project implementation in member developing countries. At present the substance of the EDI's work emphasizes macroeconomic and sectoral economic policy analysis. Through a variety of courses, seminars, and workshops, most of which are given overseas in cooperation with local institutions, the EDI seeks to sharpen analytical skills used in policy analysis and to broaden understanding of the experience of individual countries with economic development. Although the EDI's publications are designed to support its training activities, many are of interest to a much broader audience. EDI materials, including any findings, interpretations, and conclusions, are entirely those of the authors and should not be attributed in any manner to the World Bank, to its affiliated organizations, or to members of its Board of Executive Directors or the countries they represent.

Because of the informality of this series and to make the publication available with the least possible delay, the manuscript has not been edited as fully as would be the case with a more formal document, and the World Bank accepts no responsibility for errors. Some sources cited in this book may be informal documents that are not readily available.

The material in this publication is copyrighted. Requests for permission to reproduce portions of it should be sent to the Office of the Publisher at the address shown in the copyright notice above. The World Bank encourages dissemination of its work and will normally give permission promptly and, when the reproduction is for noncommercial purposes, without asking a fee. Permission to copy portions for classroom use is granted through the Copyright Clearance Center Inc., Suite 910, 222 Rosewood Drive, Danvers, Massachusetts 01923, U. S. A.

The backlist of publications by the World Bank is shown in the annual *Index of Publications*, which is available from Distribution Unit, Office of the Publisher, The World Bank, 1818 H Street, N.W., Washington, D.C. 20433, U.S.A., or from Publications, Banque mondiale, 66, avenue d'Iéna, 75116 Paris, France.

Chung-yum Kim is a former chief of staff to the president of the Republic of Korea. He has also served as minister of commerce and industry and minister of finance.

ISSN 1020-234X

Library of Congress Cataloging-in-Publication Data

Kim, Chŏng-yŏm, 1924–
    Policymaking on the front lines : memoirs of a Korean
practitioner, 1945–79 / Chung-yum Kim.
      p. cm.—(EDI retrospectives in policymaking)
    ISBN 0-8213-3014-4
    1. Korea (South)—Economic policy—1960– 2. Kim, Chŏng-yŏm, 1924–
3. Cabinet officers—Korea (South)—Biography. I. Title.
II. Series.
HC467.K4655 1994
338.95195—dc20   94-22730
                                                                     CIP

Contents

Foreword v
Acknowledgments vii
Preface ix

1. **Fruitful Years as a Central Banker** 1
   At the Bank of Chosun 1
   At the Bank of Korea 5

2. **In the Ministry of Finance as Director General of Finance** 15
   Financial Stabilization Programs 15
   Growth-Oriented Stabilization 17
   Exchange Rate Policy 17

3. **A Frustrating Year at the Korean Central Intelligence Agency** 21
   Second Currency Reform 21
   The Foreign Loan Guarantee System 27

4. **Back to the Ministry of Finance as Vice Minister** 29
   Introduction of the Foreign Loan Guarantee System 29
   Project Evaluation and Monitoring 30
   Dealing with the Stock Market Crash 31

5. **Vice Minister of Commerce and Industry** 37
   Background to Liberalization Measures 37
   Export-Promoting Industrialization Strategy 38

6. *Appointed as Minister of Finance*   43

   The Office of National Tax Administration
and Preparations for Tax Reform   43

   Joining the GATT   46

   The Establishment of the Korea Exchange Bank   47

7. *Back to the Ministry of Commerce and Industry*   49

   The End of Limited Electricity Supplies   49

   Export Promotion Policies and Their Implementation   51

   Rationale for Developing the Heavy
and Chemical Industries   52

   The Export Promotion Special Account   60

8. *Chief of Staff to President Park Chung Hee:
An Unexpected Appointment*   65

   Freezing the Informal Money Market: The Emergency
Decree for Economic Stability and Growth   66

   The Law on Facilitating the Opening
of Closed Corporations   73

   Introduction of the Value Added Tax   74

   The Urgent Need for National Security
and Industrial Policies   83

9. *Helping the President with His Strategic Projects*   89

   The *Saemaul* Movement   89

   Reforestation Projects and Policies   96

   Construction of a Network of Expressways   103

10. *President Park's Vision and Leadership*   115

   The Reunification Policy and Its Rationale   116

   Quick Decisionmaking and Prompt Implementation   116

   Innovative Ideas   116

   Personal Qualities   117

   Commitment to Social Justice and Austerity   118

   Development Strategy and Policies
and Their Implementation   120

Foreword

This new series, *EDI Retrospectives in Policymaking*, presents first-hand experiences with economic, financial, and sectoral policymaking and implementation in developing economies from the perspective of selected policymaking practitioners. In so doing, the series illustrates and brings to life the multiple competing forces at work in the political economy that influence virtually any policy decision. We are pleased to inaugurate the series with a contribution by Mr. Chung-yum Kim, who was a leading figure in economic policymaking and implementation in the Republic of Korea during its formative years and its recent high-growth period.

To ensure a well-focused presentation, authors in this series have been asked to use a specific framework for their analysis of events and processes. The framework emphasizes clarity in identifying and describing the policy issues and options in question, the rationale behind the decisions taken, how the policies were implemented, the political economy problems that may have arisen, the results of the implemented policies, and the conclusions or lessons learned during the process.

Although the series is intended primarily for officials from developing countries and economies in transition, it will also be of interest to students of development economics, political science, international relations, and area studies.

The reader should bear in mind that memoirs are by their very nature the personal recollections of a single author and are therefore subjective and colored by individual interpretation and preference. It is clearly impossible to ensure complete objectivity in the discussion of any given issue, or even absolute precision about the nature and sequence of events that may have occurred three decades ago. It is especially true in this case that the views expressed are those of the author and do not necessarily reflect those of the World Bank or its affiliates. We do believe, however, that this kind of publication can make a significant contribution to the literature, and we leave it to the reader to judge its merits.

Vinod Thomas
Director
Economic Development Institute

Acknowledgments

I would like to thank Youngnan Yu, my daughter-in-law, for translating my memoirs into English and Joon-kyung Kim, my son, for reviewing the translated text.

Finally, I dedicate this book to my beloved wife, Soon-ja Kang, who has supported me faithfully since our marriage in 1946.

Preface

I worked for the central bank of the Republic of Korea and the Korean government for thirty-four years, between 1944, when I started out as a clerk at the Bank of Chosun, the forerunner of today's Bank of Korea, and 1980, when I resigned from my post as ambassador to Japan. In 1950 I participated in the drafting of the Bank of Korea Act, and in 1953, when I was only twenty-nine, I wrote the entire text of the First Currency Reform. After that I was often involved in major Korean economic policies, either directly or indirectly.

I had considered the Bank of Korea my lifetime employer, but in 1959 I was dispatched to the Ministry of Finance. I served as the director general of the Financial Bureau through the end of the First Republic, the transition government, and the beginning of the Second Republic. From 1962 to 1969 I worked as vice minister of finance, vice minister of commerce and industry, minister of finance, and, finally, minister of commerce and industry. From 1969 to 1978 I was the chief of staff to President Park Chung Hee, and from 1979 to 1980 I was Korea's ambassador to Japan.

As for my contributions to the field of finance and banking, I was responsible for the First and the Second Currency Reforms and was closely involved in the Presidential Emergency Decree in 1972, which froze informal money markets. I also supported the introduction of a value added tax.

In the areas of industrial and social policies, I was involved in the export first and industrialization policies of the 1960s. Most of all, I was instrumental in the development of Korea's heavy and chemical industries and the build-up of the defense industry. Furthermore, I dedicated myself to various issues in which President Park showed an interest: agricultural development, the reforestation of the mountains, the *Saemaul* (new village) Movement, and the construction of expressways.

Looking back, I was frustrated more than just once or twice. In the 1950s, when I was helping to rebuild and stabilize the economy after the Korean War (1950–53), I wondered whether Korea, struggling as it was with "Asian stagnation" and the vicious cycle of poverty, could ever graduate from being a developing country. In the 1960s, when I was involved in the First and Second Five-Year Economic Development plans, I was determined to make the economy take off. In the 1970s, when Korea was becoming one of the newly industrialized economies, I recollect I worked single-mindedly, with a deep sense of achievement.

These memoirs are an attempt to record the Korean economic policies in which I was closely involved from the beginning of the 1950s to the end of the 1970s. Rather than simply follow a chronological order, I have concentrated on major policies and subjects so as to discuss the background, motivation, contents, processes, and results.

The Korean original of this volume was serialized in the *Chungang Economic Daily* from 1989 to 1990. It was published in book form in October 1990 under the title *Thirty Years of History of Korean Economic Policies— Kim Chung-yum Memoir* and in 1990 received the second Free Economy Publication Culture Award.

For the English version, the original text has been revised to eliminate details likely to be of interest only to Koreans. The focus is on issues relevant to policymakers in developing countries and transforming economies. I have emphasized my recollections of development strategies from the beginning of Korea's take-off to Korea's arrival as one of the newly industrialized economies. President Park Chung Hee oversaw this period of development, and I believe that his strong leadership contributed to the successful outcome.

1

Fruitful Years as a Central Banker

In 1941 I was admitted to Oita College of Commerce in Kyushu, Japan, without having to sit for an entrance examination. Because of the worsening situation as World War II dragged on, I graduated in September 1944, six months before the scheduled graduation date. I graduated second in the class and received the Japanese Commercial Education Promotion Director's award. On leaving college I applied for a job at the Bank of Chosun, the central bank of Korea in colonial days, and secured a position as a clerk. Thus began my career as a central banker, which was to last for about fifteen years.

My father also started his career at the Bank of Chosun after he graduated from Tokyo Higher Commercial School (now Hitotusubashi University). Later he became the president of Cho-Heung Bank, one of Korea's five major commercial banks, and was a long-time member of the Bank of Korea's Monetary Board.

Immediately on joining the Bank of Chosun, I was conscripted into the Japanese army as one of the first Koreans to be so conscripted. In 1945, at the end of the war, I returned from the army after being a victim of the Hiroshima atom bomb, and rejoined the Bank of Chosun.

At the Bank of Chosun

The atmosphere of every workplace in those days was turbulent, because of the struggles among Koreans taking over management from the Japanese. There was a movement dubbed "Expelling Koreans Who Cooperated with the Japanese." In the Bank of Chosun, as elsewhere, executives who had cooperated with the Japanese were under pressure to resign from their posts. The bank also had a left-wing group that was attempting to consolidate its power.

Immersion in Research

Instead of joining any of the factions, I decided to dedicate myself to research, feeling that I needed to learn more about contemporary economic theory than I had been exposed to at college. I frequented the used bookstores that were overflowing with Japanese books that the retreating Japanese had sold. I read late into the night to learn about how Korea should approach the currency issue. I covered the theories on central banks, currency, banking, and the gold standard, as well as histories of the Great Depression and the Bretton Woods Accord, which resulted in the founding of the International Monetary Fund and the International Bank for Rehabilitation and Development.

In 1946, for the first time since liberation, my bank held a research paper competition. I entered with a paper called "A Discussion of the Korean Currency Issue," and won a top award. In my paper I argued that the system should be freed from the metal standard and that the currency issue system should be managed. My point was that the management standard for the currency supply should depend on stabilizing prices, improving the level of employment, and maintaining the balance of payments at the optimum level, and I discussed how the central bank should manage and control such a system.

In 1947 I began working for the Treasury Department. The Bank of Chosun had handled the Chosun governor general's treasury fund and was the Bank of Japan's treasury agent during the Japanese occupation, and with the advent of American military rule, the Bank of Chosun handled the treasury funds of the American military. The Bank of Chosun took over the tax revenues the Japanese had collected, but because of postwar confusion, the amount of taxes collected was negligible, and the Bank of Chosun had to grant the government overdrafts to meet its sizable budget deficit.

Proposal for the Central Bank's Treasury Fund

In 1947, with only one year left before the founding of the Republic of Korea, one of the main tasks facing the government was to decide how to deal with the treasury fund as an independent nation.

One day I was browsing in a used book store when I found a three-volume book on the regulations governing the treasury fund at the Bank of Japan. I also found about ten books on national bonds, public accounts laws, and the public accounting systems of European and American countries. I immediately snapped up as many of the books as I could pay for and reserved the rest.

After reading the volumes on the Bank of Japan's treasury fund regulations several times, I thought I had fully grasped the topic. From other books I learned that the Japanese regulations, written during the Meiji Restoration, were based on the French system. I realized that public accounts were a specialized government bookkeeping system, quite different from commercial bookkeeping or banking bookkeeping. I drafted a proposal for the central bank's treasury fund regulations, complete with commentaries, to circulate among my colleagues at the bank. This proposal later became the foundation of the Bank of Korea's regulations. In this way, the Korean treasury fund system was indirectly modeled on the French system.

Proposal for the National Bonds Act

In 1949, when I was working for the Monetary Policy Department, I was called in to see the vice minister of finance. He informed me that the government was about to issue national bonds, and asked me if I knew much about national debt. When I said that I did, he asked me to draft a proposal. I prepared a proposal for the National Bonds Act, and submitted it along with a lengthy commentary gathered from my research on the Supreme Court cases during the Japanese occupation. My proposal was passed, without a single change on its wording, to the Ministry of Finance, the Office of Legislation, and finally, the National Assembly. The National Bonds Act was enacted on December 19, 1949, and by the end of the year, the first Korean government national bonds were issued in the amount of W10 billion (US$22.2 million).

Establishment of the Bank of Korea

With the foundation of the Republic of Korea in 1948, the Bank of Chosun organized a committee to study the central banks of various countries. I joined the committee and concentrated on currency issue systems and treasury funds. The committee outlined a proposal for the Central Banking Act, and at the end of 1948 submitted it to the government, the National Assembly, and the Economic Cooperation Administration. The government set up the Committee for Finance and Banking in the Ministry of Finance to review the proposal, and finalized it in early 1949.

The government decided to obtain an opinion from foreign experts before submitting it for legislation. In early September, Arthur Bloomfield, director of the International Balance of Payments Division of the Federal Reserve Bank of New York, and John Jensen, associate director of the Auditing Department of the same bank, came to Korea to prepare the bills of the Bank of Korea Act and the General Banking Act based on the Bank of Chosun's proposal. I was a legislation officer in charge of wording. Bloomfield and Jensen prepared a draft in February 1950 and submitted it to the Korean government, along with the signature of the Economic Cooperation Administration director in Korea. The Finance and Banking Committee in the Ministry of Finance made some changes to the proposal, which was then reviewed by a committee of officials from the Ministry of Finance, the Office of Legislation, and the Bank of Chosun. I participated in the committee as a general assistant. The most controversial problem was whether currency, banking, and foreign exchange, which according to the Government Organization Law fell under the jurisdiction of the Ministry of Finance, could be managed by the Bank of Korea's Monetary Board, of which the minister of finance was chairman and the vice minister of finance a representative.

In countries with a British-American legal tradition the monetary board, an administrative committee, is a branch of the representative body, but this is unprecedented in countries with a continental legal tradition. Therefore the discussion focused on possible violations of the Government Organization Law, and even of the Constitution. I combed the National Central Library for interpretations of monetary boards under British-American law and the opinions of Japanese public law scholars that would support our position that the existence of a monetary board is legitimate under the Korean Constitution.

After a month of heated debate, the legitimacy of Korea having a monetary board was agreed on. After revising some words in the supplementary articles, the proposal was sent to the National Assembly. More debate ensued, but representatives from the Bank of Chosun explained the sticking points. Finally the Bank of Korea Act was passed after a slight revision on April 21, and it was promulgated on May 5, 1950.

Meanwhile the Bank of Chosun set up committees to examine how to liquidate the Bank of Chosun and establish the Bank of Korea. I was an active member of these committees. On May 11, 1950, the Act for the Establishment of the Bank of Korea was promulgated. On the same day, the members of the Committee for the Establishment of the Bank of Korea were appointed and a temporary office was opened. I was closely involved with this office, handling practical matters in drafting by-laws, organization rules, and registration procedure.

From November 1945 to June 1950 I dedicated myself to the establishment of the Bank of Korea with youthful enthusiasm. Later, when I was deputy director of the Research Department, I drafted the Agriculture Bank Act, which divided the Korea Federation of Financial Associations into the Agriculture Cooperation Association and the Agriculture Bank. In 1961 these two organizations were reunited and remain so to this day.

At the Bank of Korea

With the launching of the Bank of Korea in June 1950, I was promoted to a submanager in the Research Department. Because of the Korean War, we were evacuated from Seoul, and a few days before that I was unexpectedly told that I was to be transferred to the Tokyo branch. The bank had granted me this special favor as a reward for my hard work.

Working for the Bank of Korea's Tokyo Branch

In Tokyo, I had ample time to do my own research into currency reform and the determination of the optimum exchange rate. I chose these themes deliberately in the belief that they were highly relevant to the formulation of stabilization policy in Korea. I made a special effort to understand how Japan had determined its exchange rate in 1950 and formulated and implemented its growth-oriented stabilization policies during 1945 to 1950. I learned a lot about Japanese policies from by research and, in particular, I came to understand the importance of implementing strong, dramatic policies despite public uproar about them and of having industrial policies. I came to believe that at times industrial policies are more important than finance and banking policies.

In May 1952 I was transferred to the Bank of Korea's Research Department in Seoul. I had lived in Tokyo just a little more than a year, but I came home satisfied, knowing that I had learned a great deal.

The First Currency Reform: My Research Bears Fruit

The Planning and Research Division was the flower of the Research Department. Its activities included planning for money, credit, and foreign exchange policies as well as writing annual and quarterly reports and reporting domestic trends for the Monthly Research Bulletin. Two months after my arrival in Seoul, I became the division's chief.

The Korean War was still going on, and the inflation rate was impossibly high because of the release of a large amount of currency to pay for the war. I thought a currency reform was called for to bring inflation under control and build up the country. Outside my regular duties, I wrote an insiders-only paper describing other countries' successful currency reforms after World War II. Song In-sang, the bank's deputy governor, expressed an interest in this paper. In July 1952 I was summoned by Kim Yu-taik, governor of the bank. Kim said he had read my paper with interest, and urged me to write about the necessary procedures in case Korea underwent currency reform. He emphasized that it was just an idea and that the work should be done in secret.

My Proposal

The Bank of Korea made advances of Korean currency to the United Nations forces in the form of overdrafts that were now overdue. I worked late into the night for two weeks drafting a proposal that included the importance, methods, and examples of currency reform and how to settle the overdrafts to the United Nations forces. I asserted that after the reform, the country should implement comprehensive economic stabilization policies. A few days later Kim called Song and me to his home to discuss my ideas. They asked me questions and pointed out which areas needed further work. I submitted the revised proposal at the end of August.

In early September 1952 Paik Too-chin, the minister of finance, asked me to come to his office. When I arrived I found Song and Kim already there. The minister told me that currency reform was desperately needed, and asked me if I could do the preparatory work. Without hesitation I said yes. I was given a document to sign that contained a clause that stated that I would be executed if I revealed the secret. I needed someone to work with, so I recommended Pae Soo-kon, then my assistant. Pae and I were driven in Kim's car to a private home in Haewundae, Pusan. For a while we worked in the outer quarters of the house and ate our meals out, then we moved from hotel to hotel until the reform was announced. The preparatory period lasted about six months, and about halfway through the director of the Research Department and the director of the Currency Issue Department of the Bank of Korea joined us. The former was in charge of organizing a financial institution network for each region and appointing and dispatching personnel to each region. The latter was responsible for allotting, transporting, and storing the new money and collecting the old money.

The most difficult part of our work was copying everything by hand as copiers were not yet available. Thus we wrote everything out twice to report to Song and Kim. In the beginning Pae and I did the copying, but soon the work overwhelmed us, and we enlisted the help of three bank employees.

The proposal was ready in January 1953. In early February, Mr. Reed, the finance and banking director of MacArthur's Command Headquarters who had been involved in the Japanese currency reform, flew in from Tokyo to review our proposal. Pae and I translated the whole text into English before his arrival. We were not sure if he would understand our translation, because we resorted heavily to the dictionary for a word-by-word translation. However, he had no problem grasping the meaning of the text, perhaps because he was an expert in currency reform. I spent two days with Reed answering his questions. I could not speak English well, but as I was involved in shaping the proposal from the beginning, I could understand his questions easily, and he understood my clumsy English. Reed said that the draft was excellent and predicted that the currency reform would succeed.

The Government Accepts My Proposal

There was a final discussion of the proposal with the minister of finance and the governor and deputy governor of the Bank of Korea, at which point they decided nothing in the text needed to be changed. To obtain presidential approval, the minister of finance went to see President Syngman Rhee in Seoul, bringing with him the text and the president's speech on the occasion of the Emergency Currency Decree that we had drafted. The minister returned with a presidential signature on the text, but the president wanted to write his own speech. A few days later we received his speech. It was in his own shaky handwriting, written in old-fashioned Korean. Some passages were hard to understand because of his use of outdated words, but we did not dare to make any changes. We just corrected the outmoded spelling and printed it for release around the country.

D-day was set for February 15, the day after the lunar new year. The date was set to minimize the inconvenience caused to people because they would have bought large supplies of groceries and new clothes right before the holiday. Another reason was that we wanted the National Assembly to be in recess. During the holiday assemblymen traditionally went to their constituencies. The Korean Constitution guarantees the president the right to issue an emergency decree in case of emergency when the National Assembly cannot be convened. The printing was started on February 10. The presidential speech and the entire text of the Emergency Currency Reform Decree were printed at the Mint Corporation, which was surrounded by military police. We lied to the workers' families, saying that they could not come home until a problem with the currency had been solved.

I was in charge of overseeing the printing of 500 copies of all the documents, including the president's speech, the Emergency Decree, and the enforcement ordinance. Everything was ready by noon on February 14. We loaded the documents into a truck and went to the Mijinjang Hotel, the temporary site of Reform Headquarters.

At the bank, a notice had been put up on the morning of February 14 announcing a dinner at the Mijinjang Hotel that same evening to be hosted by the governor of the bank, and stating that all male employees were required to attend. At eight o'clock, after dinner, the waiters were sent away, and the governor began to explain the background of the currency reform. Then the directors of the Research Department and the Currency Issue Department explained the details of the schedule and other practical matters. Finally, I went over the text, article by article.

Meanwhile, the minister of finance called an emergency Cabinet meeting, and obtained unanimous approval of the reform. He came to the Mijinjang Hotel afterwards and asked us for our full support. At Pusan Port, two navy ships were waiting to take the new banknotes to other parts of the country.

Back at the hotel, the bank personnel asked me question after question throughout the night, so that they would be able to provide guidance to other banks. I hoped that their journeys would be safe because it was still a tumultuous time; sometimes there were guerilla attacks in certain regions. During the implementation period, one of our teams was attacked by communist guerrillas in the countryside, but luckily no one was killed.

After the lengthy explanation, I went back home briefly to tell my wife the news, and headed for the bank to take charge of the Currency Reform Headquarters. The headquarter's main concern was to prevent people from reporting deposits in portions in different regions and to provide a uniform interpretation of the decree.

National Assembly Approves Reform

The government asked the National Assembly to convene to approve the decree, and a majority voted for the passage of the bill on February 21. The gist of the Emergency Currency Decree was as follows:

- The circulation and trading of old money was prohibited from February 17. From that date, only currency issued by the Bank of Korea was to be circulated as legal tender, on which no restriction would be imposed. The exchange rate between the new money and the old money was 1 to 100.
- Payment orders, such as old money and checks, were to be deposited in a financial institution between February 17 and 25.
- Monetary claims and debts to the banks were to be reported.
- Those who deposited payment orders, such as old money and checks, could exchange up to 500 hwan per capita for living expenses until February 25.
- For travelers, up to 500 hwan would be paid at the rate of 100 to 1, and any remaining payment orders, claims, and debts were to be

reported to the financial institution in their home district by February 25, accompanied by a traveler's exchange document. If travelers could not report by the due date, they could report or submit the old money later with the permission of the minister of finance. Special considerations would be given for medical and funeral expenses.

Implementation

The Emergency Currency Decree was implemented without a hitch. The moneyed class complained about the limits imposed on their purchasing power. At that point, we learned that President Rhee had questioned why there were restrictions on money. We held an emergency meeting at the bank. If money was to be exchanged without limit, the program amounted to no more than a change of currency denomination, and it would be useless in reducing the excessive purchasing power concentrated in certain groups, which was the source of wartime inflation. We decided to keep the president's doubts secret, while the minister of finance and the deputy governor of the bank would go to Seoul to explain once again the text the president himself had approved. I was to go with them, but in the end I remained in Pusan to deal with the questions that were continuously pouring in. Considering President Rhee's stubbornness, I knew that persuading him was likely to present an immense obstacle.

On a windy, rainy day the minister of finance and the deputy governor of the Bank of Korea flew to Seoul in a light army airplane. In Pusan we worked through the night, anxious about the outcome. The next day we heard the good news that the president had agreed to continue with our original plan. The unexpected crisis was over, but I sometimes wonder if President Rhee understood the essence of the currency reform as a special economic policy.

Second Stage of the Reform

The Emergency Banking Decree, the second stage of the currency reform, was sent to the National Assembly on February 25. The gist of the Emergency Banking Decree was as follows:

- To curb spiraling inflation and stabilize the economy, a certain portion of the frozen deposits were to be transferred to the special time deposits or the special national bond deposits that took one to three years to mature at annual interest rates of 4.8 to 5.0 percent. The remainder was to be transferred to free accounts that could be drawn on without any restrictions.
- To encourage savings in the future, preferential rates were to be given to prereform deposits in the following order: long-term deposits, demand deposits, and deposits of the currency in circulation at the time of transfers from frozen accounts to free accounts
- In transferring into the special time or special national bond deposits, progressive rates were to be applied to different amount brackets with a certain amount of basic deduction (a large amount would be more disadvantageous than a smaller amount).
- Projections indicated that the special time and special national bond deposits would total 3 billion hwan (300 billion old won), equivalent to about one-third of the currency in circulation before the reform. The hope that wartime windfall profits would be leveled out in the process.

Opposition to the Decree and the Revised Proposal

As soon as the decree was presented to the National Assembly, the outcry of the moneyed class, especially wartime profiteers, was loud. The opposition party wanted to revise the text of the reform extensively. The Liberal Party (the ruling party) was the majority, but was split into two factions because of the vice president's nomination (the vice president was to be President Rhee successor's. Since the Korean constitution specifies that, in the event of the president's death, the vice president has the right of succession.

The minister of finance explained the administration's position clearly, while Bank of Korea executives approached the assemblymen one-on-one in an attempt to persuade them. However, the bill was eventually defeated and had to be drastically revised, because a ruling party faction sided with the opposition party. As a result, the total amount transferred to the special time and special national bond deposits was 1.3 billion hwan instead of the 3.0 billion hwan originally projected, and the contraction effect on the money flow was 2.2 billion hwan. However, the prospect for settling overdrafts to the United Nations (UN) forces, another purpose of the reform, was bright. As the president revealed in his speech on the reform, there had been an unwritten agreement between Korea and the United States that the United States would clear overdue overdrafts if the Korean government had a resolute policy to overcome inflation.

U.S. Representative Praises the Reform

On February 25 Admiral Herren, the U.S. representative of the Korea-U.S. Combined Economic Board, flew from Tokyo to Korea to talk with the minister of finance, the board's Korean representative. Herren praised the reform, and suggested that the United States pay the overdrafts to the United Nations forces, which amounted to US$86.8 million, using an exchange rate of W6,000 to the dollar. As a result, the foreign exchange reserves for the new money were secured, and a large quantity of materials could be imported to restore old factories or construct new ones. The two governments agreed that the overdrafts to the UN forces would be paid monthly so as to suppress inflation.

Studying at Clark University Graduate School

In 1956 I was appointed deputy director of the Research Department. Around that time, I began to want to study contemporary economics in a systematic way. The bank paid tuition if an employee chose to study abroad, and three employees had already taken advantage of this benefit. I decided to be the fourth. With my supervisors' approval, I started the application process and got hold of some textbooks widely used in American graduate schools. I began to pore over them one by one.

In December 1957 I left for Clark University in Worcester, Massachusetts, to begin the January semester. Although Clark was a small school with an enrollment of only 2,000, it was one of the 60 major schools in the United States, and its graduate school, which opened in 1882, was the second oldest graduate school in the United States. The head of the economics department was Professor James A. Maxwell, a well-known scholar in public finance and fiscal policy. He asked me how soon I was planning on finishing my master's degree. I answered two years, but he advised me to take only three courses during the spring semester instead of the usual four. I was secretly hoping to finish the program sooner than the usual two years, however, because I had left my wife and four children behind. I told him I wanted to take four courses.

I read about 100 pages every day. Because I could not read English very fast, it took me about ten hours, and I would stay up until two o'clock in the morning. The only exceptions were Friday nights, when I had dinner with other Korean students and went to see a movie or drink beer, and Saturday mornings, when I did grocery shopping and laundry.

After a semester, I was told that I would get a tuition exemption and a monthly stipend of US$45 for books. I took two courses in the summer, and started writing a thesis entitled "The Korean Economy from 1945 to 1957," having secured Maxwell's approval. During the fall semester, in addition to the normal course load, I wrote my thesis and I submitted it to Maxwell chapter by chapter. He would return my drafts with his comments and editing. By the end of December my draft and my course work were finished.

I went to see Maxwell in January 1959 to get some advice about the courses I could take while revising my thesis. He handed me the final chapter of the draft and asked me when I was planning to go home. I had expected to be revising my thesis until at least the summer, so I was taken aback. Until then he had never praised me, but now he smiled and said I had done a good job and all I had to do was to have it typed for submission. I was at a loss for words, so I just kept thanking him. A week later, I handed in the typed and bound thesis and received a paper certifying that I finished my master's requirements.

I came home at the end of January. Thinking back, it had been a difficult year. I did not like Western food, so I had cooked Korean dishes in my room, washing the ingredients in the wash basin and cooking them on an electric burner. I did not want to spend too much time cooking, so I made enough rice and soup to last a few days. The main side dishes were kimchi, dried pollack, and seaweed sent from home. I had also found it hard to understand some professors who had southern or European accents. During tests I could not write in fluent English, so I had to be satisfied with writing down the main points and a conclusion, skipping an introduction and other frills. For assignments I did my best after thorough research, and as a result my papers were often praised during class.

I gained new knowledge during this period, but I was more glad that I could develop a systematic framework for the information I had accumulated over the years through random reading. In a sense, I had been shown a direction for lifelong, self-directed study.

Professor Roger C. Van Tassel, the professor of macroeconomics and international economics, encouraged me to pursue a Ph.D. However, I returned home, knowing that I had been sent to graduate school to finish a master's degree and that my goal was not to become a scholar.

2

In the Ministry of Finance as Director General of Finance

On March 20, Song In-sang was appointed as minister of finance, and he asked me to work for him as director general of finance. In those days, director general of finance was a rank equivalent to deputy governor of the Bank of Korea. There was strong opposition to my appointment in the administration as I was only the deputy director of my department at the bank. I had to sit a test given to prospective government officials, and discovered that they had made the test especially difficult. Nevertheless, on April 10, 1959, I became the eighth director general of finance.

Financial Stabilization Programs

The combined U.S.-Korean Economic Board was established in May 1952 and included the Financial Committee, headed by the Korean minister of finance and the Subcommittee, headed by the Korean director general of finance. In 1957 the United States called for the adaptation of the Financial Stabilization Program, which periodically projected budget disbursement and bank loans, in return for continued economic aid. The American side, although traditionally respectful of Laissez-faire and market forces, suggested instituting emergency measures to curb inflation, which was running at more than 30 percent a year. The Korean government had no choice but to comply with the program that the Finance Committee planned and executed.

The most important and difficult part of the director general of finance's job was to plan and execute monthly, quarterly, and annual financial stabilization programs and to maintain or negotiate the official foreign exchange rates. The Financial Stabilization Program became more detailed every year, and by 1959 it had taken on the characteristics of a state-controlled economy in the finance and banking sectors. The monthly, quarterly, and annual stabilization programs were divided into the public, banking, and foreign sectors. The public sector included not only the government's general accounts, but also the revenues and expenditures of all special accounts. The banking sector comprised investments and working funds for major manufacturing entities, as well as all kinds of policy funds and seasonal loans for farmers and fishermen, while the foreign sector dealt with exports, imports, and sales of government reserve dollars.[1]

The aim of the program was not simply to predict trends or design policy guidelines; it was a detailed execution plan for finance and banking. If adjustments were likely to be needed, agreement had to be reached between Korean and U.S. representatives. The Finance Committee reviewed the plan's execution every month and every quarter, thus the planning had to be accurate and thorough, and the execution had to be done with caution.

Even the National Assembly approved a budget for a certain item, if it did not appear in the monthly or quarterly Financial Stabilization Program, the funds were not disbursed during that period. As the quantity, terms, and conditions of policy funds were closely related to the success or failure of policy projects, each ministry and office made an all-out effort to secure funds. The American side, emphasizing economic stabilization, often demanded what amounted to domestic intervention. In other words, trying to keep stability while allocating funds according to priorities was a balancing act.

Fortunately, I was well equipped with knowledge about industry gained from the surveys I had conducted while at the Bank of Korea's Research Department. For the execution of the plan I only paid attention

---

1. To help, for example, agriculture, fisheries, and small and medium-size businesses despite limited government funds, the government asks the banks to make loans in compliance with government policies, and on preferential terms compared to regular bank loans.

to the total sum for each category, leaving the details to each ministry, institution, and bank.

Growth-Oriented Stabilization

In my new position I focused on checking the ever-expanding currency, keeping the currency on an even keel by the quarter. However, my goal was to expand production facilities, electricity and coal supplies, and the support given to small and medium-size industries. I also wanted to support agriculture by increasing the number of loans using rice as collateral.

In 1959 the main focus of the Korean economy was the completion of fifty-one new projects, most of which were factories aimed at import substitution. These factories were started in 1954 or 1955 as postwar restoration projects, and I did my best to have them completed and to support those small and medium-size businesses the Ministry of Commerce and Industry recommended. However, remarkable results were hard to come by because of various problems, including the lack of capital, insufficient accumulation of technological know-how, unsatisfactory management skills, and insufficient electricity. In addition, the government, the public, and businesses were unaware of the importance of economic development, and the country lacked strong leadership.

The years 1957 to 1960 were a period of economic stability. Inflation, which had been running at more than 30 percent per year during 1953–56, was lowered to 2 to 3 percent a year between 1957 and 1960 thanks to the effective execution of the Financial Stabilization Program.

American aid peaked in 1957, and from then on project aid (investment aid) was gradually reduced, while program aid (grains and fertilizers) increased. The decrease in project aid meant that the GNP grew by only 3.9 percent in 1959 and 1.9 percent in 1960. In other words, during my years as the director general of finance, Korea achieved stabilization, but growth was minimal.

Exchange Rate Policy

The foreign exchange rate was a chronic headache for the ministers of finance in the years after the Korean War. President Syngman Rhee had a stubborn belief about foreign exchange, and foreign currency could be spent only with his approval. He believed that an appreciated exchange rate maximized foreign exchange earnings from the overdrafts to the United Nations (UN) forces and increased amount of aid. If devaluation occurred, he blamed the Ministry of Finance for its incompetence. The following paragraphs describe how successive ministers of finance tried to appease the president:

On February 25, 1953, right after the currency reform, the Combined Economic Board set the exchange rate for the overdrafts to the UN forces at 180 hwan to US$1, with the provision that the rate would be adjusted every three months based on the price index. In August 1953 the UN demanded that the exchange rate be devalued to reflect the skyrocketing price index, but the Korean administration would not concede. On October 1, 1953, the minister of finance stopped accommodating the overdrafts to the UN forces as a means of pressuring the UN, and the UN forces retaliated by not supplying imported oil to the Korean side through Korea Oil Storage Company (KOSCO), which was under the UN's sole management.

When the dispute was settled, the UN forces' expenses were supplied in hwan after auctioning foreign currency through the Bank of Korea. The foreign exchange rates became multifaceted: the official rate, the UN forces' auction rate, the auction rate of U.S. aid dollars, and the free market exchange rate for export dollars. In 1955, U.S. and Korean representatives met to try to set a single exchange rate. The American side contended that a realistic rate was 700 hwan to US$1, while the Korean side insisted on 360 hwan to US$1, which was the weighted average of the auction rate of U.S. aid dollars. Finally the two sides agreed on a compromise on August 12, 1955, setting a single exchange rate at 500 hwan to US$1. In September 1956, an agreement was signed that stipulated that if the price index rose more than 25 percent, the rate would devalue automatically.

By April 1959, two and a half years later, the wholesale price index had risen almost 25 percent. Because President Syngman Rhee was obstinate about not devaluing hwan, the minister of finance's main task was maintaining the existing rate. He directed me to do everything in my power to keep the existing exchange rate. In principle, the exchange rate denotes the external value of a country's legal tender, so it is only rational that the policy to maintain the foreign exchange rate is equivalent to a price stabilization policy. I not only tried to control total demand, but also paid attention to the supply and demand situation in many individual areas. I was not content with the wholesale price index report sent by the

Bank of Korea every ten days. I asked the bank to report the index every morning to help me draw up a plan. I was extremely busy, mobilizing the finance and banking resources that I supervised and enlisting other ministries' cooperation in the use of transportation and aid funds, the adjustment of import items, and the implementation of regulatory actions against hoarding.

How to finance grain and fertilizer was a controversial issue, not only in the government, but also in the National Assembly. Presidential approval was required to sell reserve foreign currency to pay for imports needed for a more effective price stabilization policy. As President Rhee believed that the amount of foreign currency reserves equaled the wealth of a country, Minister Song had a hard time obtaining his permission to sell foreign currency.

In some ways, my job was broader in scope than the director general of finance's job, because I also had to do things that were actually the responsibility of the price director. Despite the ministry's efforts, the wholesale price index rose more than 25 percent in early 1960, warranting an adjustment of the exchange rate. On February 23, the rate was set at 650 hwan to US$1. Personally, I thought a drastic devaluation was called for to ensure interim stabilization for a longer period, but nothing could be done against the president's wishes.

The presidential election of March 15, 1960, was generally known to be corrupt and unlawful, and as a result protest rallies took place all over the country, culminating in a student uprising on April 19. President Rhee was forced to resign, and on April 28 an interim government was set up. I intended to return to the Bank of Korea after minister Song's resignation. However, the new minister asked me to stay on until the new government took office.

The interim government handed over power to the new administration on August 19, 1960. When the new minister was appointed, I wrote a letter of resignation telling him I wished to return to the Bank of Korea. The minister wanted me to wait until my replacement was found, so it was not until September 16, 1960, that I officially resigned. However, the new minister asked me to complete the financial stabilization plan for the last quarter and to prepare the following year's plan. I insisted that as someone who had resigned I could not do this, but the vice minister pleaded with me, saying the year's end was the most demanding time for currency and fund matters, while conceding that for a minister to ask such a favor of an employee who had resigned was unusual. I reluctantly decided to cooperate. I stayed on in a temporary office for about a month to draft a stabilization plan and made sure that an agreement was reached with the United States. Finally I returned to the Bank of Korea in October.

3

A Frustrating Year at the Korean Central Intelligence Agency

In October 1961, a Korean Central Intelligence Agency (KCIA) man came to see me and asked me to come and help the agency with economic policies. I was reluctant to assume this responsibility; however, the governor of the bank told me that he had been officially asked to send me to the KCIA. Clearly I could not avoid the summons unless I resigned from the bank. I started going to the Policy Research Room at the KCIA as an adviser. Other advisors were there who were specialists in diplomacy, the Constitution, politics, administration, sociology, economics, and so on. My job was to write papers about pressing economic problems.

Second Currency Reform

In 1962 I was called in to the minister of finance and introduced to General Yoo, who was in charge of economic matters for the military government as a member of the Supreme Council. The general said that he had heard about me, and asked me to write an article about currency reforms in other countries and Korea's experience with its 1953 currency reform, for which I had drafted the full text. Claiming that my article would be purely for reference, he took me to a secret room near the City Hall, where I worked for about a month. On completion of the work, Yoo asked me if I would be interested in becoming a minister at the Korean Embassy in

Washington, D.C. I said yes. I started the necessary procedures for the move at the end of March, and my departure date was set for early May.

Preparing the Proposal

One day in April, Yoo called me in again and asked me to draw up a concrete proposal for currency reform, stressing that no decision about instituting such a reform had been made yet. I recommended five colleagues who had worked with me on the first currency reform. We had our first meeting at a secret KCIA house. We were told that Korea needed to generate investment funds through a currency reform to ensure a successful launch of the First Five-Year Economic Development Plan. We thought that traditional finance and banking methods were more effective for supplying industrial funds. However, as we had already pledged to keep the matter a secret and were under special orders, we decided to work on the proposal and point to traditional financial and banking measures as an alternative. We submitted the completed proposal and the alternative measures in early May. I heard nothing further, so I started packing and prepared to leave for the United States.

Explaining the Proposal to the Coup's Leaders

On May 17 I was summoned to see Park Chung Hee, the leader of the successful military coup of May 16, 1961. Several generals were present. When asked to explain the proposal, I first explained that a currency reform was unnecessary to supply industry with funds, but that sufficient preparation was a must if currency reform was decided on. I then explained the details of the proposal and the alternative measures. The generals said that considering the banks' old-fashioned attitude and their management based on collateral, they could not be relied on exclusively for supplying funds required for the First Five-Year Economic Development Plan.

I explained that the first currency reform had succeeded because there had been prior agreement with the American aid authorities for the smooth receipt of aid before and after the reform. I insisted that as long as we were an aid recipient, close cooperation with the United States was required for stockpiling aid materials before the reform and for smooth receipt of aid afterwards. Everybody agreed on this point, and Yoo assured us that he would take care of the matter. The generals said the proposal for the reform was excellent, that a new batch of banknotes would arrive in Pusan Port the following day, and that D-day would be June 10. I was speechless. I was ordered to go to Pusan to help unload the new banknotes.

On May 18, 1962, I met three KCIA men at an American military airport. We flew to Pusan and then headed for the dock. We found a Dutch cargo ship anchored there, and several Korean airborne unit officers were waiting for us with their men. Soldiers began to unload the cargo. There were six kinds of new banknotes, ranging from W1 to W500 notes packed in wooden boxes with metal seals. The boxes were so large and heavy that it took four soldiers to lift one. The boxes were stacked in areas marked with signs indicating various military supplies. The unloading alone took two days. Afterwards our main worry was whether the ship's crew would reveal the secret as the ship was on its way to Japan. We discussed it with an English man who was in charge of the transportation of the banknotes, and he assured us that only three men on the ship knew about it, and that we had no reason to doubt their professionalism. I left for Seoul, leaving the soldiers behind to guard the cargo for the following twenty days until the day of the currency reform.

As soon as I got to Seoul I gathered my group from the Bank of Korea, informed them about the arrival of the banknotes and that the reform was scheduled for June 10. Everybody was surprised, but started to work on the final review and preparations for the reform.

Decisions Taken Before the Proposal

According to accounts published by Yoo and the Korean ambassador to the United Kingdom, the need for a currency reform had been decided on July 22, 1961, to generate domestic capital for the First Five-Year Economic Development Plan. The idea was to freeze the idle capital held by the moneyed class, forcibly diverting it to the Industry Development Corporation, which would invest the funds in certain enterprises until they could stand on their own feet. Afterwards, investment would be funneled into other enterprises in turn. The Industry Development Corporation would also guarantee foreign loans for the enterprises.

The minister of finance had visited the United States with President Park in November 1961, and on his way home he had stopped in several countries to inquire about the possibility of printing banknotes, but without a prototype banknote, he could not sign a contract. That same month, when the minister of commerce and industry was on his way to Europe for an official visit, he was asked to take a picture of Korea's Independence Gate to the United Kingdom. While there, with the help of the Britsh Ministry of External Affairs, he contacted a printing company. In February 1962, when Yoo asked me to write a paper on the currency reform, the new banknotes, with pictures of the gate on them, had been already ordered.

On June 9, 1962, the Supreme Council, the Cabinet, and the governor of the Bank of Korea gathered to pass the Second Emergency Currency Measure. A speech by the Supreme Council's chairman was released that pointed out the need for the currency reform. The atmosphere of the meeting was heated, but after my presentation many members told me that I had done a good job. The banknotes were transported to the Bank of Korea's offices that night, and were distributed to various financial institutions. A headquarters for the Emergency Currency Measure headed by Yoo was set up at the Bank of Korea.

Discussion with the United States Ambassador

On June 10 the U.S. Ambassador to Korea and some of his staff paid a visit to the Bank of Korea to meet Yoo, the minister of finance, and the bank's governor. I was present at the meeting. The ambassador expressed regret that there had been no prior consultations with U.S. representatives about the reform despite America's large volume of economic aid. He then praised the execution and the efficiency of the process, but demanded consultations before the Emergency Banking Measure (the second-stage measure) was put into effect. Yoo replied that the matter had not been discussed with the United States for security reasons, and that he would confer with the United States before the second measure was implemented. I was surprised to learn that Yoo had not informed the United States about the currency reform, but was relieved by his promise.

I had with me a copy of an English translation of the first currency reform. I gave it to Yoo, explaining that if a new translation outlining the differences between the first and second reforms was added, preparing the English text should not be too difficult. Yoo said he would take care of it, and I dedicated myself to the main problems at headquarters.

On June 16, the first day of the Emergency Banking Measure, heated argument broke out at the Supreme Council meeting held to pass the measure. The members of the Financial Committee criticized Yoo for not consulting with them before the announcement, but in the end the measure was passed and proclaimed. At the same meeting, the entire Cabinet resigned.

The gist of the Emergency Banking Measure was as follows:

- A certain percentage of payment orders, such as old banknotes and checks, reported and submitted by a natural person, a juridical person (corporation or company), or an organization was to be diverted to the frozen accounts, while the rest was to be converted to free accounts without any payment limit.
- Demand deposits would be treated in the same way as payment orders.
- Regular savings accounts, installment savings accounts, money trusts, and postal savings with a maturity of more than one year would be converted to free accounts.
- A certain percentage of the installment savings with maturities of less than a year would be frozen, while the rest would be converted to free accounts.
- A 15 percent annual interest rate would be applied to the frozen accounts, which would be replaced by shares of the Industrial Development Corporation, to be established within six months of June 18, and at the time of the conversion to stocks the government would guarantee a 15 percent annual dividend rate. Afterwards, the stocks would be listed on the stock exchange and could be sold any time.

Opposition to the Emergency Banking Measure

When the Emergency Money Measure was proclaimed, the United States Embassy and the United States Operations Mission expressed strong displeasure, because the government had not entered into any prior consultations as promised. According to Yoo's memoir, he was asked for a meeting many times, but refused one. A reshuffling of the Cabinet was announced on June 18.

When the outburst of the Supreme Council members and the displeasure of the United States Embassy became public, the business sector's fury grew.

I was kept busy drafting countermeasures to alleviate the situation and to return it to normalcy. When the money market was normalized, the Currency Countermeasure Headquarters was disbanded.

United States Disapproval of the Reform Measures

Even after the Emergency Banking Measure was proclaimed, no dialogue took place with the United States Embassy, and the attitude of its staff stiffened noticeably. The embassy's position was that freezing savings accounts with maturities of less than a year was unreasonable.

Countries only carry out currency reforms in rare political situations, such as after a war or a revolution. The United States has no history of currency reform, thus it was only natural that except for a few experts, American economists did not approve or know much about currency reform. The former Federal Republic of Germany was an exemplary case of successful currency reform after World War II, which laid a foundation for that nation's future economic development. It was planned by three American experts under the Allied occupation by freezing the money supply, including currency in circulation, demand deposits, and a certain portion of savings accounts, thereby curbing inflation and supplying industrial capital without increasing the amount of currency issued.

President Park Complies Despite My Strong Opposition

I submitted a paper to the U.S. Embassy referring to the example of the Federal Republic of Germany and explaining that freezing a certain portion of savings accounts was reasonable. However, the Americans insisted on cancellation of the freeze on deposits of less than one year maturity (15 percent of total deposits), and Park Chung Hee decided to comply with their demands despite my strong opposition, judging that it would make little difference to the overall outcome. Accordingly, part of the deposit freeze was eliminated on June 30. However, the Americans were still not satisfied, and demanded the removal of the entire freeze on deposits. In other words, they demanded the cancellation of the currency reform, threatening to stop economic aid if Korea did not comply. American economic aid accounted for a large segment of Korean economic management, and furthermore, a severe crop failure was expected in 1962. Although Korea was an independent country, it was difficult to withstand American pressure.

Looking back, conflict between the United States and Korea had arisen right after the 1961 military coup, and even after the United States recognized the military government, the relationship between the two countries was far from cordial. When the currency reform was done without any consultation with the United States and rumors abounded that Korea was turning to state capitalism, the United States must have felt that a confrontation was in order.

Second Currency Reform Was Misconceived

The Supreme Council was reshuffled and Yoo resigned from the council. I drafted a new bill on the frozen deposits in which one-third was to be converted to free accounts, while the rest was directed to the special savings accounts with a maturity of one year. This measure was proclaimed on July 13. The second currency reform ended in failure, merely denominating old money to one-tenth of its former value, and unnecessarily interrupted the workings of the national economy. Among the various economic policies I have been involved in during my 34 years of public life, the second currency reform stands out as a bitter disappointment.

The Foreign Loan Guarantee System

When I had to take action to remove the restrictions on deposits in July 1962, I strongly recommended that Chairman Park introduce a foreign loan guarantee system to facilitate funding for economic development, and accordingly he took prompt action. By the end of the month the foreign loan guarantee system had been enacted. Korean businesses were to work out loan agreements with foreign lenders, and the Korea Reconstruction Bank (later the Korea Development Bank) and the Bank of Korea were to guarantee the loans after approval by the Economic Planning Board and the National Assembly. (In later years, commercial banks were authorized to issue the guarantee and the Korea Exchange Bank took over the responsibility for guaranteeing the foreign exchange convertibility of loan payments from the Bank of Korea.) By eliminating most of the risk for foreign lenders, the Korean financial authorities opened the door for massive borrowing abroad.

4

Back to the Ministry of Finance as Vice Minister

After the Currency Countermeasure Headquarters was disbanded, I prepared to go to the United States to work at the Korean Embassy in Washington, D.C. On June 28, 1962, the day of my departure, I went to say good-bye to Park Chung Hee, the chairman of the Supreme Council. He told me that the new minister of finance wanted me to become his vice minister, and asked me to report to work immediately. This I did after completing my work on the second currency reform in July 1962. Becoming vice minister of finance caused a big change in my life. I had been dispatched to the government by the Bank of Korea before, but the vice minister of finance was a representative of the Monetary Board, which supervised the management of the Bank of Korea. Therefore I could not possibly remain as a Bank of Korea staff member. This was a major turning point in my life. Kim Se-ryun, the minister of finance, used to work for the Bank of Korea, and was not only a financial expert, but was also conversant with stocks.

Introduction of the Foreign Loan Guarantee System

The minister and I both supported the financial aspects of the First Five-Year Economic Development Plan that had started that year. However, we were faced with an acute shortage of domestic savings, and hence were seeking foreign capital. A single private entrepreneur could not secure a loan individually from the international capital market. Moreover, the U.S. aid authority was planning to terminate grants by 1965 because Korea was considered hopeless in terms of economic development. It was in this context that I had proposed to President Park, before I became vice minister, that Korea adopt a foreign loan guarantee system, and President Park had not only agreed with the proposal, but had implemented it within the month (see chapter 3).

Despite strong opposition by many Koreans to the introduction of foreign capital for fear of economic colonization, President Park (formerly chairman of the Supreme Council) supported the idea because he believed that it would generate positive externalities for the country. Specifically, the introduction of foreign capital would provide Korea with a chance to obtain technical skills and managerial know-how as well as easier access to world markets. Furthermore, he stressed that investments in large companies by friendly countries would be helpful for national security. He ordered the pertinent government ministers and vice ministers to find out the difficulties foreign entrepreneurs were encountering so that they could be corrected.

Project Evaluation and Monitoring

President Park monitored the progress of every single project, both public and private, and closely governed the industrialists by the stick and carrot method. The government held monthly and quarterly meetings to evaluate projects and examine economic trends. Such regular meetings were chaired by the president and attended by senior government officials, ruling party leaders, and bankers. (In later years labor union leaders and representatives of industrial associations were included.)

The president established a situation room next to his office in the Blue House to keep abreast of progress. With frequent phone calls he encouraged government officials to complete assigned projects. The Ministry of Finance provided a sizable number of preferential loans through the banks to enterprises that did not have enough collateral, while ministries supported them through preferential allocation and transportation of construction materials. The president believed that even private projects in the First Five-Year Economic Development Plan should be completed as scheduled, because the government fully guaranteed the foreign loans so that they would not become burdens on the government, and ultimately on the Korean public.

The plan was examined and revised every year, with each ministry doing its best to accomplish its assigned annual targets. Although the Korean economy was a free market economy, it embodied some characteristics of a planned economy when it came to the development plans.

Dealing with the Stock Market Crash

Another concern for the ministry was the May 1962 stock market crash. When I took up my post, investors thronged the ministry every day asking for a solution. However, before discussing the crash let us review the history of Korea's stock market.

Early History

The first Korean stock exchange, the Chosun Exchange, was established in 1932. The Chosun Exchange was a joint corporation whose origins were the securities market in Seoul and the rice and bean exchanges in Inchon. The Chosun Exchange had its headquarters and stock department in Seoul and a commodity exchange in Inchon. In 1939 a government-owned company took over the commodity exchange, making the Chosun Exchange the real stock exchange. In 1943 the Chosun Exchange was made a public corporation in an effort to rid it of problems resulting from its private management. The act specified that the purpose of the stock exchange was to ensure fair price formulation and smooth circulation of stocks, and that the government was to appoint its director. In 1945 when Japan was defeated, the Chosun Exchange closed its doors because of the postwar sociopolitical confusion.

After liberation, the first stock exchange opened on March 3, 1956, with the establishment of a public corporation. As the law for the stock market had not yet been prepared, it was based on the Chosun Exchange Act of the colonial years. In December 1953, an attempt had been made by the National Assemblymen to pass a stock exchange bill for the first time, but this failed because it was presented too late in the National Assembly session. In 1954 the Ministry of Finance asked the Monetary Board for advice on drafting the stock exchange bill, and then proposed it to the National Assembly.

My Proposal for the Stock Exchange

In 1954 I was the director of the Bank of Korea's Planning and Research Division. I drafted a proposal in which I recommended the establishment of a public corporation in which financial institutions, the insurance industry, and the government invested. I also favored taking whatever measures were necessary to prevent speculation by banning futures transactions. After deliberation, the Monetary Board sent my proposal to the government.

Stockbrokers' Opposition

The Ministry of Finance revised the bill to give the stock exchange a choice of whether to be a private or a public corporation, perhaps because of the strong lobby by the brokerage houses in favor of a private corporation. The stock exchange bill was repeatedly defeated at the National Assembly, and in April 1959, when I was director general of finance, it was still pending. In June 1959 the Finance Committee of the National Assembly began to deliberate the bill in earnest, focusing on whether the stock exchange should be a public or a private entity. The minister and I insisted that a public corporation under the government's strict supervision was a must to prevent rampant speculation, while the stockbrokers asked for a private cooperation.

In 1960 the stockbrokers were still pushing for a private corporation. In April the student uprising took place, and in August a new government came into power. The newly appointed minister of finance was one of the assemblymen who had originally proposed a bill in 1953 under which the exchange would be a private corporation. The stockbrokers saw their opportunity, and while briefing the minister, I began to worry that he might favor the private corporation plan.

My Skepticism about the Need for a Stock Exchange Bill

Personally, I did not think the passage of a bill, even for a public corporation, was urgent. Stock investment comes of age only when per capita GNP and savings are high enough. In those days the per capita was less than US$100, and because the banks were chronically overextended, they relied on the Bank of Korea for their resources. Furthermore, in terms of the stock supply, practically no firms showed stable profits. Some people claimed that strong promotion of the stock market was necessary to mobilize the domestic capital required for economic development. However, I firmly believed that the required capital could be borrowed from foreign countries, and that the required domestic capital could be derived from the funds of the Korea Reconstruction Bank and from rolling over commercial bank loans. I believed that Korea would not be mature enough for a stock market for five to ten years. Therefore, I thought that the stock exchange legislation would merely convert the old Japanese act into a Korean one.

As director general of finance I explained my position to the minister, and he said that he would consider the matter of the stock exchange only when other more urgent matters, such as tax reform, the foreign exchange rate, and interest rates, were settled.

The Flawed Stock Exchange Act of 1961

With the military coup of 1961, the Supreme Council was established, and its Finance Committee reviewed some of the pending bills. The Stock Exchange Act was passed based on the private corporation plan, and even permitted futures transactions. It was proclaimed in January 1962 to become effective on April 1. The stockbrokers began to speculate, taking advantage of future transactions. Powerful politicians joined in the action and small investors followed suit. Some stock prices soared to eighty-eight times their original price. Some people became millionaires overnight, while others went bankrupt when the market collapsed. The stock exchange listed its own stocks at twenty-nine times their face value, which was what eventually caused the market to collapse. The Monetary Board decided to dedicate W28 billion for the settlement of buying and selling transactions at the exchange, in addition to the W10 billion already released, but some transactions had to be nullified. The stock market was closed after the currency reform on June 19.

Minister Kim and I had the market reopened in forty days, and tried to curb speculation. Although the number of transactions decreased, speculators were as active as ever, causing smaller crashes in August and November. In 1963 a strong restraint policy was implemented, and speculators abandoned the market. Stock prices kept falling, and clients asked for the market to be temporarily closed.

Minister Kim Se-ryun resigned on February 25, and I also submitted a letter of resignation because I was sick and tired of stock matters. However, my resignation was not accepted, perhaps because of the scarcity of people conversant with the stock exchange.

Restructuring the Stock Exchange as a Public Corporation

I judged that restructuring the stock exchange as a public corporation was the only way to lay a foundation for the development of the stock market. As long as it was a private corporation, I believed that excessive speculation and collapse were likely to happen again. However, obtaining the approval of the new minister of finance was not easy, because he had been on the advisory board of the Finance Committee when the structure of the stock exchange had been discussed. He seemed to feel that overturning a Supreme Council decision might compromise its authority. Only after repeated requests from me did he approve the proposal.

I drafted a plan in which the government and the banks invested W500 million each to buy the stock exchange's stocks at a price lower than their face value as a way to compensate small holders of stocks. The stocks held by others would be bought successively as the exchange's management was normalized.

We immediately started to negotiate with the Economic Planning Board for the government's investment, but received a negative response. We gave a briefing to the head of the Cabinet, but he also said it would be better to leave the exchange closed for the time being in the belief that it was nothing but a source of problems. The Finance Committee of the Supreme Council was also reluctant to make the change. Finally, we reached an agreement in which the government and the banks would invest W300 million each the following year.

President Park Approves

Now we needed approval from Chairman Park Chung Hee. We were told that he abhorred even the word stock and although we asked for a meeting with him for a long time we were not granted an appointment. Finally, a briefing was arranged. I was nervous because how well I presented my case could determine his approval. Chairman Park listened without a change of expression, and afterwards asked other Supreme Council members whether they agreed with my proposal. When they all expressed positive opinions, he gave his approval.

The Stock Exchange Act was revised on April 27, and the opening ceremony was held on May 8 with an investment of W300 million by the banks. The government investment followed two years later. The stock market opened the next day, May 9, and I resigned from my post on June 3. Buying and redeeming all the stock exchange's stocks took ten years. In 1963 fifteen firms had listed stocks, and by 1972 the number had increased to sixty-six. Thanks to various policies, such as the implementation of the Emergency Decree of 1972, which froze the informal money market, the 1973 Corporation Opening Promotion Act, and the 1974 Presidential Special Directives, by the end of 1979, 309 large firms had gone public and 355 were listed on the stock exchange. By 1989, 625 firms were listed, making Korea one of the ten major stock markets in the world in terms of quantity.

5

Vice Minister of Commerce and Industry

On June 12, 1964, I was appointed the vice minister of commerce and industry without prior notice. I was told later that they announced it without obtaining my prior consent because they knew I would refuse if given the chance. I was embarrassed and confused. The post at most would last a year or two, could I refuse it after the announcement? I accepted the position with mixed feelings.

Background to Liberalization Measures

When I became the vice minister of commerce and industry, Korea's economic conditions were as described in the following paragraphs.

The size of Korea's territory, 99,400 square kilometers, was a quarter of that of Japan, and 60 percent of it was mountainous. Of the total land, 10 percent was developed as residential areas and 30 percent was arable land. Two-thirds of the arable land was dedicated to grains, with rice making up half the grains grown. Korea was not self-sufficient in food and animal feed, and despite its mountainous terrain, the country's natural resources were limited.

The population in 1964 was 29 million, and Korea was one of the most densely populated countries in the world. Korea's education level, by contrast, was relatively high, with almost everybody having at least elementary schooling and the illiteracy rate close to zero.

The Korean War had destroyed almost all production facilities, and starting in 1953, the economy was restored with American aid. From 1953 to 1960, American economic aid amounted to US$2.1 billion, which successfully restored production facilities to their prewar levels. Most industries were processing industries that took advantage of aid materials, such as wheat, sugar, timber, and wool. In addition, some import substitution industrialization was under way that was heavily protected by a quota system, import restrictions, import prohibitions, tariffs, an overvalued exchange rate, and a very low interest rate.

Industrial production recovered quickly, reaching a level higher than the peak of the prewar years by 1956. In 1960 the industrialization rate was 16 percent; however, excessive investment in facilities caused a recession because of the small domestic market. The average growth rate for manufacturing between 1954 and 1956 was 17 percent, but between 1958 and 1961 the rate dropped to 6.9 percent.

In terms of trade and foreign exchange, from 1956 foreign exchange holdings were on the increase, but after 1962 they began to decrease. At the end of 1962, gold and foreign exchange holdings stood at US$167 million, a decrease of US$39 million from the year before. In 1963 foreign exchange holdings continued to decrease, and in June 1963 they were at US$114 million, a US$56 million drop from the end of 1962. Alarmed by this trend, a feeling of crisis prevailed, prompting the implementation of the export-import link system, a measure to increase exports and limit imports. In early 1963, materials needed to manufacture items for export and for the Five-Year Economic Development Plan were excluded from the export-import link system. In July 1963, however, with few exceptions all items were placed under the export-import link system. An export subsidy system had also existed since 1961, and a barter system was in operation for certain export items.

In June 1964 the need to transform these import substitution policies to export-oriented ones to break the stagnation became urgent. However, under the protection policies the import-oriented and import substitution industries were much more profitable than export-oriented industries.

Export-Promoting Industrialization Strategy

The government took strong liberalization measures starting in 1964. The exchange rate was fixed at W65 to the dollar in the late 1950s, devalued to W255 in May 1964, and in March 1965 a single floating system was adopted. A drastic readjustment of interest rates was put into effect in 1965, for example, the realistic deposit interest rate in 1964 (taking price increases into account) was -8.4 percent for a one-year deposit, but in 1965 it was raised to 17.3 percent. The liberalization of imports fell under the jurisdiction of the Ministry of Commerce and Industry. The Minister, Park Choong-hoon, left the means and methods of liberalizing imports and fulfilling exports goals for the year to me, and the following paragraphs describe my focus.

Import Liberalization and Exchange Rate Policy

I started by canceling the export-import link system that was in effect at the end of 1964. Next, I increased the number of automatically approved import items, which stood at zero in June 1964, to 8.0 percent of total items approved for import during July–December 1964 and to 62.7 percent in December 1965. I delegated the administration of import approval to the Bank of Korea. In November 1964 I eliminated many import quota items to lay a foundation for the single floating exchange rate. Finally, in January 1965, as a preliminary measure for the implementation of the floating exchange rate, I eliminated outdated policies, including export subsidies, the import-export link system, and the barter system with the exception of barter specified in trade treaties. The floating exchange rate was finally implemented on March 22, 1965, when the conditions were deemed right.

The ministry divided imports into the following categories: automatically approved, approved, and prohibited. Import transactions were limited to letters of credit, documents against acceptance, or documents against payment. Import approval was switched from the positive list system, which only allowed those imports on the list to a negative list, which prohibited the importation of items on the list. This change became effective in July 1967 when I was the minister of finance.

In 1967 tariffs were lowered. For example, the tariff for nondurable consumer materials was reduced from 74.2 percent in 1966 to 43.2 percent in 1967.

Special Measures for Export Promotion

In addition, special measures were implemented to promote export industries. I believed it was important to select industries suitable for

Korea's circumstances that could bring about quick results so that the focus could be shifted to other industries. In July 1965 thirteen products were selected taking into account such factors as their comparative advantage, the effect on the international trade balance, the effect on employment, and finally the ripple effect on other industries.

The products selected were raw silk, cotton, ceramics, rubber, radios, electrical appliances, canned seafood, canned mushrooms, wool, plywood, clothing, leather, and crafts. These items received technological support and financial support from domestic loans and foreign exchange. Government officials were appointed to oversee these industries and act as troubleshooters. The policy worked well. For a considerable time these items became Korea's major exports, giving Koreans a boost of confidence.

Implementation of the Strategy

Until I was promoted to minister of finance in January 1966, I was filled with a sense of accomplishment practicing those policies I believed in. The Ministry of Commerce and Industry had two major fields of administration: trade and mining and manufacturing. The administrative duties for these two areas often contradicted each other. To solve the inherent conflicts I held directors' meetings every morning, explaining to them the background theories for trade liberalization as well as the founding motives, goals, and functions of the International Monetary Fund and the General Agreement on Tariffs and Trade. I emphasized that we needed to take a step toward liberalization despite the uproar within the business sector. I also asserted that we needed to move away from the processing industries toward the heavy and chemical industries. I explained that protection policies were necessary in the take-off stage, but that enterprises should be thrust into free competition as soon as they could stand on their own feet.

However, the directors' attitudes did not change overnight, partly because almost all the divisions had counterparts that had conflicts of interests within the ministry and also in the business sector. For example, the Export Department had to fulfill export goals while the Import Department had to control imports to prevent a foreign exchange crisis. I discussed the topics at the directors' meetings and dealt with them one by one. Because the ministry often required quick decisions, sometimes loud debates ensued during the meetings. Division chiefs also attended the meetings to air their concerns. When the debates were finished, I tried to come up with a fair decision in light of the trade liberalization and industrialization policies.

The export goal for 1964 was US$120 million, for the first time set over US$100 million. Many people believed that the goal was too high, but the Ministry of Commerce and Industry did its best to succeed. In early November the minister of commerce and industry left on a long tour of Europe with an economic delegation. I encouraged the staff to reach the US$100 million mark by November 30. On December 31, I collected and added numbers until late into the night, and when the figures were ready I called the president, who was delighted with the achievement of the goal.

6

Appointed as Minister of Finance

On January 25, 1966, I was appointed the minister of finance, and I set myself three goals: (a) to implement a financial plan to stabilize currency values and distribute funds efficiently, (b) to improve the tax administration and the preparation of tax reform, and (c) to join the General Agreement on Tariffs and Trade (GATT) and establish a foreign exchange specialty bank to support the continued expansion of exports.

The year was 1966 when the First Five-Year Economic Development Plan was finished and the Second Five-Year Plan was to be prepared. The demand for funds was growing, and the key to Korea's economic development and stabilization depended on how funds would be supplied.

The Office of National Tax Administration and Preparations for Tax Reform

Tax revenues, the key to mobilizing domestic capital, could be increased in two ways: reinforcing the tax administration and reforming the tax system. I believed that by establishing the Office of National Tax Administration (ONTA), tax collection would increase by 20 to 30 percent, even without reform.

However, the previous regimes had been very conservative about expanding the government, and public opinion was against administrative expansion. Adding offices or divisions to the government was not something that could be done easily. One such new office, the Office of Fishery, was about to be founded following the signing and ratification of a treaty and agreement with Japan in December 1965 to promote the fishing industry and raise fishermen's incomes. The studies for founding the ONTA began around the end of 1965, when the view that such an institution was necessary was growing.

As soon as I became minister of finance, I was briefed by the Subcommittee for the Establishment of the Office of the National Tax Administration. The subcommittee could not agree on whether local tax offices should remain, or whether the decisionmaking and personnel management should be handed over to the ONTA. To this point, the director general of the Tax Bureau in the Ministry of Finance headed the Tax Administration and, except for a few senior positions, had the right to manage tax personnel. If the ONTA were to be an independent entity, its head would be at the same rank as the vice minister, and the ministry would no longer have the right to manage tax personnel. Thus, senior ministry officials were not happy about creating the ONTA. However, believing that a strong ONTA was essential, I decided to push for its foundation. I quickly decided on a plan that allowed the continued existence of the local tax offices and assigned the personnel management, except for a few senior positions, to the administrator of the ONTA. Although the minister of finance was to have political responsibility for the ONTA, its administration was to remain with its administrator.

The Cabinet and the National Assembly passed the law amending the Government Organization Law, and the Office of National Tax Administration opened its doors on March 3, 1966.

Tax reforms had taken place several times since the establishment of the Korean government in 1948, but the tax administration had never been changed. Before the establishment of the ONTA, the tax institutions consisted of the Tax Bureau in the Ministry of Finance; four local tax offices in Seoul, Taejon, Kwangju, and Pusan; and seventy-seven collecting offices and two branches nationwide. The ONTA now had tax supervisors, planning and management officers, the collecting bureau, the direct tax bureau, the excise tax bureau, the research bureau, the tax research bureau, the assessment bureau, and the general affairs bureau. Tax inspection and investigation duties were greatly reinforced. Accordingly, the foundation for improving and developing the tax system had been laid.

I supported the new ONTA administrator so that he could work independently. He announced that he would increase tax collection to W70 billion, a 50 percent increase, and make tax administration as nondiscretionary as possible by eliminating corruption, tax evasion, and arbitrary tax assessment procedures. He was chosen for the post because as a presidential secretary he had investigated tax evasion by some firms. The business sector seemed worried about whether a large-scale tax inspection would ensue.

I believed that the tax administration's job was to encourage taxpayers to report their incomes correctly by educating them and minimizing their resistance to paying taxes by using reasonable management. I asked the administrator to guide and educate the taxpayers as best he could.

The tax officers made efforts to collect personal business income tax, corporation tax, commodity tax, and business tax, and as a result, without resorting to tax inspections, tax collection increased to W74 million in 1966, a 68.7 percent increase compared to the previous year, and W104 billion in 1967, a 47.6 percent increase. These figures include natural increases derived from economic development, but they also indicate a considerable level of tax evasion in previous years. Years later, in 1984, when I visited the East-West Center in Hawaii as a visiting fellow, I heard that the center had recently held a seminar for Asian economists to study Korea's successful tax administration.

In the ministry, the post of assistant minister in charge of tax was created, and the Tax Bureau became the Tax System Bureau. While the ONTA dealt with tax administration, the Tax System Bureau focused on research and legislation to improve the tax system.

In early 1966 when I became minister, the tax system was inadequate: tax revenues were insufficient for the demands of the First Five-Year Economic Development Plan. In addition, because of the excessively high direct tax rate and the steep progressive rate, people in the higher tax bracket were eager to reduce or evade their taxes. Income, corporation, and inheritance taxes were subject to the progressive tax, whose rate went up to 70 percent, much higher than that in most other countries. The steep progressive rate had been created over the years, not only based on the principle of income redistribution, but also because of political pressure on the National Assembly to lower the rate for those making less money. The difference in revenue was passed back to the higher bracket to make up.

I believed that tax reform was called for. The plan was to draft a proposal by the end of 1966 that would be put in effect in 1967. The process included a fundamental review of the direct tax, including personal business income tax, corporation tax, and inheritance tax, as well as a revision of a set of other taxes, including business tax, registration tax, liquor tax, commodity tax, and telephone tax.

In September 1966 I had to resign from my post when I took moral responsibility for a saccharin smuggling scandal that shook Korea that year, when one of the large conglomerates smuggled in saccharin when building a fertilizer plant with foreign credit. The next minister took over the tax reform, but the revisions did not fully reflect the original plan, so the change in the steep progressive tax rate was not implemented. My only regret is that I had to resign before the reforms I had envisioned bore fruit.

Joining the GATT

The GATT is an international trade organization in which almost every free country participates. The advantages of joining the GATT were as follows:

- A multilateral treaty would help avert the need to sign separate trade treaties with other member countries, which would support the development of Korea's overseas market In addition, GATT provisions would not discriminate against Korean products.
- The concession tariff rates for 66,000 items, which had gradually been lowered in the meetings of member countries, would be applied to Korean products, thereby increasing their competitive edge.
- The GATT would provide access to up-to-date trade information.

Despite the advantages, Korea could not have joined the GATT before because of the various trade barriers Korea imposed on imports, such as the export-import link system, the quota system, the barter system, and the export subsidy system. When the ONTA was founded, the customs organization was restructured by adding an International Division to deal with GATT-related matters. The trade liberalization measures were being carried out one by one, and the preparation for the shift from the positive to the negative list system was almost finished.

At the GATT the Kennedy Round, which required a drastic lowering of member countries' tariff rates, was on the verge of being concluded. I judged the time was ripe for Korea to join the organization. There was, however, strong opposition from the Agriculture-Fishery Committee at the National Assembly. I often went to their meetings to try to change their minds.

On May 20, after Cabinet approval, I applied for admission to the GATT. Soon we started concession negotiations so that Korea could join the organization as soon as possible. The negotiations at the GATT's Geneva headquarters went smoothly for sixty items, and Korea joined the organization in April 1967. On May 15, 1967, Korea participated in the Kennedy Round, getting a 35 to 50 percent tariff decrease on eighteen concession items. It is not an exaggeration to say that by joining the GATT Korea laid the foundation for successful export promotion.

The Establishment of the Korea Exchange Bank

When the Bank of Korea became the central bank, all foreign exchange business was conducted by the Bank of Korea, which shared foreign exchange management with the government. However, with the increase of trade, the need arose for commercial banks to deal with foreign exchange. In February 1962, the Ministry of Finance approved five commercial banks for processing some foreign exchange business for the Bank of Korea as of April 1, 1962.

With the First Five-Year Economic Development Plan, exports grew more than 40 percent per year, and naturally the foreign exchange business increased. The international department of the Bank of Korea could not handle the extra work load efficiently, but the five commercial banks were too immature to be upgraded to the level of the Bank of Korea. Korean banks also needed to open overseas branches, but opening more overseas offices of the central bank was not the answer. Furthermore, the Bank of Korea did not handle domestic commercial banking. Thus enterprises had to use the Bank of Korea for foreign exchange and other commercial banks for trade banking. Finally, normalization of relations between Korea and Japan was imminent, and Japanese banks were expected to open in Korea based on the reciprocity principle. Thus I was determined to establish an international-level commercial foreign exchange bank that would facilitate foreign exchange transactions as well as trade banking. Such a new bank could compete with foreign banks by establishing an overseas network.

The Korea Exchange Bank Act was enacted in July 1966. The Bank of Korea invested in the new bank, handing over the assets and liabilities of its foreign exchange business and transferring trained personnel. After a preparatory period, the Korea Exchange Bank opened its doors on January 30, 1967.

The Korea Exchange Bank later grew to have twenty-six overseas branches and agencies and seven subsidiaries throughout the world that supported Korean exports and supplied the foreign currencies required for the Second to the Fourth Five-Year Economic Development plans. It grew in Korea as well, with 186 branches nationwide.

About twenty years after the foundation of the Korea Exchange Bank, other banks' foreign exchange business and their ability to supply foreign exchange had matured. By 1987 some people had begun to think of the option of putting the Korea Exchange Bank under private management, and in December 1989 the Korea Exchange Bank Act was abolished. In January 1990, twenty-three years after its establishment as a specialty bank, it became a private commercial bank.

7

Back to the Ministry of Commerce and Industry

On October 3, 1967 I was playing golf when to my surprise a messenger arrived to inform that I had been appointed the minister of commerce and industry.

The End of Limited Electricity Supplies

As the new minister, the first thing I paid attention to was the extreme shortage of electricity. Soon after liberation from Japan in 1945, the Democratic People's Republic of Korea, where most power plants were concentrated, stopped sending electricity to the south, resulting in the Republic of Korea having a dire shortage of electricity. To make matters worse, the Korean War in 1950 destroyed most of the power plants and supply facilities in the south. During the American aid period, priority was placed on investing in power plants. Restrictions on the supply of power to factories and homes was abolished for the first time in April 1965, nineteen years after liberation.

However, the supply had to be temporarily limited again in June through July 1967. In September, one month before I took office as minister, electricity had to be severely controlled again. The First Five-Year Plan for the Development of Electricity, which began in 1962, called for almost doubling the supply by 1966 from 360,000 kilowatts before the plan. However, in 1966, with an annual demand hike of 20.5 percent, the supply looked precarious, with electricity reserves at only 16,000 kilowatts. In 1967 the situation grew worse with a huge jump in demand. In November 1967 demand stood at more than 860,000 kilowatts, while the maximum supply capacity was 770,000 kilowatts.

In September 1964, the Thomas Survey Team, recommended by the U.S. Agency for International Development, visited Korea and suggested reducing the original electricity development plan devised by the U.S. Operations Mission to Korea and the Korean government. In response, the planned increase in electricity was reduced by 224,000 kilowatts. The team also recommended an annual increase of 11.9 percent from 1967 to 1971, the period of the Second Five-Year Plan for the Development of Electricity. However, the government, foreseeing the demand increase, set the annual growth rate in the Second Five-Year Economic Development Plan at 15.4 percent. The unprecedented economic development during the First and Second Five-Year Economic Development plans, especially the dramatic industrial development, brought about an electricity demand hike of 20.5 percent in 1966 and 33.5 percent in 1967. During the Second Five-Year Economic Development Plan electricity demand grew at 29.6 percent per year.

The lack of investment in electricity production was highlighted by a severe drought in 1967, which worsened the shortage of electricity. At the end of 1967, all hydropower plants, which ordinarily produced 200,000 of the total 870,000 kilowatts of power, were idle.

Electricity can not be imported into Korea or stored, and building an electricity plant takes longer than building any other facility. The only solution was to save electricity. A movement to turn off one light at each home was started, and supply limits had to be imposed. All street lights except for security lights were turned off, and display windows were allowed to have only one light on. As for production facilities, we encouraged them to operate during the night when residential electricity demand was lower.

However, the basic problem could only be solved by increasing the supply. I worked night and day to try and increase the supply by even just hundreds or thousands of kilowatts. I pushed to have the power plants under construction completed ahead of schedule, including the Kunsan Thermoelectric Power Plant (75,000 kilowatts), the Hwachon Hydroelectric Power Plant (27,000 kilowatts), and the Pusan Thermoelectric Power Plant (105,000 kilowatts). In addition, gas and diesel turbine power generators were imported via airlift to speed things up. The early completion efforts paid off: by the end of August 1968 generating capacity had increased by 202,000 kilowatts, and by the end of 1968 an additional 155,000 kilowatts had been added, resulting in a total of 1,274,000 kilowatts. By August 1968 supply restrictions could be lifted.

During this period homes and factories suffered tremendously. I visited the supply headquarters of the Korean Electric Corporation every night on my way home, and went up to the pavilion on Namsan Mountain to see how lights were being saved in the city. At the end of 1967, when the shortage was at its worst, people were even using locomotive diesel engines and engines from retired electric trollies to generate electricity. After the shortage had been eased, I decided to do everything in my power to prevent a similar situation from happening again.

As developing electrical resources required an immense amount of capital, the budgeting authority tended to keep electricity reserves at a minimum. One of the reasons for the shortage in 1967 and 1968 was attributable to a reserve capacity hovering at about 10 percent of the total supply. In meetings with the president and other ministers, I insisted that at least a 20 to 40 percent reserve was necessary, and that the necessary investment had to be made well in advance of needs. Luckily, President Park supported my idea, and an electricity resource development plan was implemented, thus Korea did not have to face the same level of shortages again.

Export Promotion Policies and Their Implementation

Throughout the 1960s the government dedicated itself to promoting exports by promoting medium-size and small industries and improving export support and administrative systems. The Ministry of Commerce and Industry prepared complex export promotion policies each year. The major policies were as follows:

- Reducing business income taxes and corporate taxes by 50 percent for export incomes;
- Introducing tariff exemptions for materials imported to make products for export;
- Providing financial support through low interest loans;
- Establishing the Korean Trade Promotion Corporation to collect information, develop overseas markets, and establish a firm under the Korea Foreign Trade Association to help small exporters;

- Expanding export manufacturing industries;
- Awarding medals and prizes to people contributing to exports (skilled workers, engineers, and salespeople) by revising the National Prize and Decoration Law.

I planned policies based on these main points between 1967 and 1970. A series of slogans was introduced: in 1967 the slogan was the "expansion of the foundation of export industries," in 1968 "the establishment of mass production systems for the export industry," and in 1969 "the modernization of export industry facilities."

I also promoted the improvement of quality, design, and packaging and the training of skilled workers. The export goal of US$360 million in 1967 was not reached; exports fell short by US$1 million. However, in 1968 and 1969 the goals of US$500 million and US$700 million, respectively, were reached without a problem.

The policy that supported the promotion of exports most effectively was the monthly export promotion expansion meeting, led by the president since 1965. Trade-related ministers; representatives from business, financial institutions, and shipping companies; and labor union leaders participated in these meetings to review export trends by item and country and to discuss problems. By means of these meetings, export promotion policies were systemized one by one. In line with the president's belief in the importance of exports the government, export companies, and support institutions pushed hard to lay a foundation for exports, and as a result exports grew continuously.

The export industrialization policies focusing on labor, intensive goods resulted in the expansion of exports and, ultimately, high economic growth. Between 1965 and 1969 exports grew at an annual average rate of 37.3 percent, and the GNP grew 10 percent per year. Exports accounted for 14.9 percent of the GNP in 1969, compared to 5.7 percent in 1965.

Rationale for Developing the Heavy and Chemical Industries

The majority of Korean exports were nothing more than products of a processing industry. Generally speaking, when more final goods are exported and more producer goods are imported, eventually a country reaches the effective minimum production scale, which gives birth to the heavy and chemical industries that produce intermediate and capital goods. The foreign currency thus saved can be invested in other producer goods, ultimately advancing the heavy and chemical industries. In 1967, when I became the minister of commerce and industry, the time was ripe to introduce heavy and chemical industries. Pohang Integrated Steel Mill and Wulsan Petrochemical Complex were built as two major projects during the Second Five-Year Economic Development Plan (1967–71). The steel mill was built under the supervision of the Economic Planning Board with the cooperation of the Ministry of Commerce and Industry, while the Ministry of Commerce and Industry supervised construction of the petrochemical complex with the cooperation of the Economic Planning Board.

The Construction of Pohang Integrated Steel Mill

In 1967, the first year of the Second Five-Year Economic Development Plan, a group called Korea Integrated Steel Associates (KISA) was formed, consisting of eighteen companies from the Federal Republic of Germany, Italy, the United Kingdom, and the United States (France joined later), and headed by an American company, Koppers. On October 10 the Korean government and KISA signed a basic contract covering the construction of an integrated steel mill with an annual production capacity of 600,000 tons. The KISA tried to proceed by obtaining loans from the International Bank for Reconstruction and Development (IBRD), the American Export-Import Bank, and the public loan authorities of various countries, but the negotiations went nowhere.

THE IBRD IS NOT RESPONSIVE. The International Bank for Reconstruction and Development (IBRD) considered that building an integrated steel mill in a developing country was bad judgment. After World War II, some of the leading developing countries, such as Brazil, India, Mexico, and Turkey, constructed integrated steel mills so as to become more economically independent. However, their 1-million-ton facilities got into trouble because of technology, management, and scale problems.

Eugene Black, president of the IBRD, had given a speech during a joint annual assembly of the IBRD and the International Monetary Fund in which he stated that three mythical keys to success in developing countries existed: building a highway, constructing an integrated steel mill, and erecting a monument to the head of state. In other words, he had expressed the IBRD's position against building a steel mill in a developing country. The KISA could not secure loans despite its best efforts, and by the end of 1968 constructing an integrated steel mill in Korea based on the KISA plan seemed impossible.

NEGOTIATIONS WITH JAPAN. In August 1968, a regular cabinet-level meeting was to take place in Tokyo between Korea and Japan. President Park gave the deputy prime minister and me a special order to start negotiations for Japanese cooperation in building a steel mill. In the Japanese government structure, the Economic Planning Office merely predicts general economic trends and sets the direction of economic development, while the Ministry of Foreign Affairs is responsible for overseas economic cooperation, and the Ministry of International Trade and Industry (MITI) is in charge of heavy industry. The Korean deputy prime minister started the negotiations at the Combined Meeting of Diplomacy and Economic Planning, while I brought up the topic during a separate meeting of representatives of Korea's Ministry of Commerce and Industry and Japan's MITI.

During a three-day session, the participants covered the regular meeting issues as quickly as possible to leave time for the topic of Japanese cooperation in the construction of an integrated steel mill. The MITI minister was Masayoshi Ohira, a confidante of Prime Minister Hayato Ikeda, who later became prime minister himself. Ohira and I had several official and private meetings in the presence of Shoichi Akazawa, who was in charge of heavy industry at the MITI.

Ohira's opinion was as follows:

- An integrated steel mill is a venture in which the principle of economy of scale is applicable. In other parts of the world, countries were building steel mills with capacities of 8 to 10 million tons, so Korea's planned capacity of 600,000 tons was inconceivable in terms of competition.
- Enormous amounts of domestic capital are required to build infrastructure such as ports, engineering works, water supply systems, roads, and railways.
- Even if Japan supported the project with the maximum possible amount of public loans and Korea could raise low interest capital domestically, the small-scale facility would not be able to produce steel at international price levels. If steel were to be produced for domestic use, it would not be economical because the Korean

machine, shipbuilding, construction, and other industries would have to use the expensive steel.

Ohira stressed that this was his frank opinion, and was unrelated to Japan's intention to sell its steel to Korea. I countered that the scale of production could be raised to a capacity of 1 million tons, and that the national budget could support the social overhead capital needed for such facilities as ports, water supplies, and roads. As for foreign exchange requirements, I asserted that part of the no-interest claims fund agreed on between Korea and Japan could be funneled into the construction of the steel mill.[1] The domestic demand for steel would be great enough, because the capacity of the rolling mill facilities was close to 1 million tons. I insisted that unlike other developing countries, Korea could build an internationally competitive, profitable integrated steel mill. I explained that we had approached other countries first because Koreans still had hard feelings against Japan, but if the Japanese cooperated in this project, the Korean people might gain a better impression of Japan, which would improve the relationship between the two countries.

Ohira conceded that if part of the foreign exchange requirement was derived from the Japanese no-interest fund, and if domestic funds were allocated from the government budget, the project might be economically feasible. However, he said that it was hard to express the Japanese position about cooperation when Korea had not yet terminated negotiations with other countries.

I asked Ohira to send a survey team to Korea to review the project, and he assented. He was a man of few words, but I had the impression that he had a favorable attitude toward our suggestion. The communiqué that was released after the meeting recorded that the Japanese government showed a deep understanding about the construction of an integrated steel mill in Pohang, which was scheduled to be finished by 1972, and had promised to send a survey team to study the possibility of cooperation.

---

1. There were timeconsuming negotiations between the Korean and Japanese governments on how to clear claims held by Koreans against Japan, namely, Japanese currency, deposits in Japanese banks, Japanese bonds and stocks, and so on. Finally, the two governments agreed that Japan would set up a no-interest fund, low-interest public and bank loans, and suppliers credit in the amount of US$300 million each, that would not be cleared on a case-by-case basis.

The next morning, before flying home, I invited MITI's director general of heavy industries for breakfast and asked his opinion about the proposed steel mill's prospects. He said that if domestic capital were derived from the national budget and part of the foreign exchange requirements came from the no-interest fund, it was worth considering.

DECISION TO BUILD WITH JAPANESE ASSISTANCE. When we returned to Seoul, the deputy minister and I reported to the president that Japan seemed to have a positive attitude toward cooperation. He directed us to conclude the KISA deal as soon as possible, and if it made no further progress in securing loans, we had better sever the ties with KISA and enlist Japanese cooperation.

In April 1969 at the third International Economic Cooperation for Korea meeting, held in Manila, the IBRD officially refused to invest in the Pohang Integrated Steel Mill. In May the American Export-Import Bank officially rejected our loan application. President Park was determined to build an integrated steel mill with Japanese cooperation, and came up with the following points to solve the problems of feasibility, the stumbling block in the loan negotiations:

- The mill's capacity would be 1 million tons.
- A significant amount of the necessary foreign exchange requirements would be funneled from the no-interest claims fund and credit assistance agreed at the claims to Japan meeting to reduce the burden of interest payments.
- The government would pay for the construction of infrastructure, such as ports, engineering works, roads, and railways, to reduce construction costs.
- With the enactment of the Steel Promotion Act, the mill would receive special considerations with regard to taxes, tariffs, and various utility bills.

FINANCING OF THE PROJECT. After the government had decided on its position, a Japanese delegation visited Korea in September 1969 to review the project, and an IBRD delegation arrived in November. The IBRD representatives stated that normal practice was to include the costs of infrastructure in construction expenses, but the Korean government convinced them otherwise by explaining that the government's investment was justifiable because constructing infrastructure would benefit not only the steel mill, but the economy as a whole. The IBRD representatives acknowledged the mill's economic and technological feasibility after various working-level meetings and a tour of the site.

The no-interest claims fund and low interest credit assistance from Japan amounted to US$300 million each, and various interest groups, such as independence fighters and fishermen, demanded shares. President Park, knowing there would be an uproar among the public, still decided to invest a considerable amount in the mill, believing that its construction would eventually benefit everyone. The total foreign exchange requirement necessary for the construction as devised by the Korean and Japanese governments was as follows.

No-interest claims fund	US$30,800,000
Public loan at 3.5 percent interest	US$46,428,000
Japan Export-Import Bank loan at 5.875 percent interest	US$52,498,000
Supplier's credit at 6.5 percent interest	US$38,332,000
Total	US$168,058,000

IMPLEMENTATION. The construction of the railway, port, water supply, and civil engineering works started in April 1968, and the 1.03-million-ton mill was started in April 1970 and finished in July 1973. The Pohang Integrated Steel Mill, supported by various tax and utility bills incentives as well as government financing, and benefiting from its employees' concerted efforts, showed a profit from its first year of operation.

PROFITS RETAINED FOR EXPANSION. The initial capital of W14 billion was invested by the government and Taehan Chungsok (the Korea Tungsten Mining Company), a rare profit-making government-invested firm, at a ratio of three to one. Loans from banks and the government were converted to stocks, but dividends were not paid until 1983, and in the intervening years were used to expand the facilities. By May 1981 production capacity had reached 8.5 million tons.

Steel is a basic material for all industry, and is especially important for the defense industry. The steel industry is divided into three processes: pig iron manufacture, steel production, and rolling. To have a competitive edge in the world market, the optimum production scale should be between 8 and 10 million tons, and processes should be automated. Korea was a rarity among developing countries in managing to operate a successful integrated steel mill.

Wulsan Petrochemical Complex

In October 1967, as soon as I became the minister of commerce and industry, I found out that the construction of petrochemical factories planned by individual entrepreneurs was not going well. I devised a plan in which the government would build a petrochemical complex and transfer individual factories to private owners.

The petrochemical industry can be divided into three processes: cracking petroleum to produce basic materials such as ethylene, propylene, and benzene; combining these basic materials to produce polyethylene, polypropylene, acrylnitro, and so on; and processing the combined materials into synthetic fabrics, synthetic rubber, and plastics.

Korea had been importing the materials to make synthetics for domestic and overseas markets. As the total amount imported exceeded the effective minimum production scale, the construction of a naphtha cracking center was planned as one of the major projects of the Second Five-Year Economic Development Plan.

FEASIBILITY STUDY BY ARTHUR D. LITTLE. From February to August, Arthur D. Little, an American company, conducted a survey to assess the feasibility of a petrochemical complex in Korea. In July 1966 the Petrochemical Division was created in the Ministry of Commerce and Industry. The most pressing question was whether Korea, as a latecomer to the petrochemical industry, could compete with established countries, especially nearby Japan. The petrochemical industry is an installation industry in which economies of scale are of great importance. If various components produced during the naphtha cracking process cannot be used, they must be burned, resulting in low economic feasibility.

The Arthur D. Little report concluded that even though there was good potential for a petrochemical industry in Korea, the demand was still weak. It suggested a 32,000-ton naphtha cracking factory to produce ethylene and eleven downstream factories.

THE DECISION TO BUILD. As advanced countries were already operating 300,000- to 500,000-ton factories, clearly a plant with a capacity of 32,000 tons would not prove to be competitive. The government decided on a 100,000-ton capacity, the internationally recognized minimum optimum size at that time, with a plan to increase capacity eventually to 150,000 tons. In September 1966 twelve downstream factories were decided on, and private companies were selected for the construction and management of these factories.

The larger a factory's capacity, the more cracked components it creates. To prevent economic failure, the downstream factories had to be completed at the same time as the naphtha cracking center to maximize the use of the cracked components. However, as mentioned earlier, the enterprises in charge of construction had made no progress in negotiating foreign loans. I decided to cancel those designated enterprises that showed slow progress and to select new ones. They protested, threatening lawsuits, but I stuck to the new plan.

IMPLEMENTATION. The government-sponsored Korea Petroleum Corporation took over the naphtha cracking center, and Chungju Fertilizer, a government-invested company, became responsible for the utility center and the polyethylene, vinyl chloride monomer, acrylnitro, and caprolactam factories. Only five facilities remained with their original private enterprises.

Completing twelve factories simultaneously was not an easy job, and neither was selecting the best production method for each facility. As the industry was progressing in leaps and bounds, various methods had been developed and patented, with each foreign factory and engineering and construction company using different methods. We took various aspects into consideration, including productivity, the operation rate, and safety, as well as the terms and conditions of loans, trying to determine which methods were the most advantageous.

Foreign and domestic companies that did not make the ministry's list petitioned the Blue House, complaining about unfairness in the selection process. President Park called me to ask my opinion about the petitions. Although there were often cases that left room for doubt, I stuck to my decision and the president always supported me.

In July 1968 I visited Washington, D.C. for ministerial-level discussions between Korea and the United States, at which joint ventures and foreign loan contracts for most of the twelve factories were under consideration. After the official meeting we visited the headquarters of some American companies in an effort to stimulate investment in Korea. We flew to Midland, Michigan, to the Dow Chemical Company and met with company executives. In addition, we spent ten days meeting executives of many other companies, and quickly succeeded in securing loans.

By October 1970 the naphtha center was finished along with nine downstream factories, and the rest were completed within a year or two. With the simultaneous launching of these major factories, the cracked components could be put to use at the maximum level, and the complex, despite its small scale, proved profitable from the beginning. Korea became one of the leading Asian countries in the petrochemical industry. Domestic demand could be satisfied and the foundation for healthy exports had been laid. Later more factories were built in the complex, further improving its economic feasibility. In the 1970s another petrochemical complex was built in Yochon, making Korea one of the advanced countries in the petrochemical industry.

The Export Promotion Special Account

In September 1989 the fifty-five-story Korea World Trade Center opened, complete with four-storied exhibition halls, a hotel, a department store, and an airport terminal. I was invited to a celebratory reception as a former minister of commerce and industry, and was told by Korea Foreign Trade Association officials that the Export Promotion Special Account, created in 1968, had been the cornerstone of this magnificent center.

In 1968 the Korean export industry and enterprises were in their fledgling stage. In 1968 exports reached a value of US$350 million, an elevenfold increase over 1962, but achieving the export goals of US$500 million in 1968 and US$700 million in 1969 required an all-out effort. Export promotion policies were urgently needed to dispatch sales missions to overseas markets, stage expositions and exhibits in Korea, send delegations to overseas functions, develop packaging and product design, and modernize test equipment for exports examination institutes.

The Ministry of Commerce and Industry tried to secure the funds needed, but the national budget was too meager to provide funding for successful policy implementation. The working-level officials at the ministry suggested a plan whereby a certain percentage of imports would be taxed and the revenues would be earmarked for the export promotion budget. This plan was inspired by the fact that a certain percentage of the tax for Bunker C oil was being used to promote the coal industry, with good results.

Some other countries were taxing imports to support export promotion, but as a latecomer in the export competition, Korea was in no position to demand that other countries eliminate such visible and invisible barriers as import tax, boundary tax, and import surcharges while Korea raised its own. I believed we should find a source of funds other than an import tax. In July 1968 I reported to the president that we would like to generate an export promotion fund, and he responded positively, asking me to discuss the matter with other ministries.

Budget authorities and tax authorities frown on an object tax because it introduces rigidity into fiscal management. As a former Ministry of Finance official, I was not in favor of such a tax, but I believed the creation of a similar policy was inevitable considering the situation. I discussed it with the minister of the economic planning board and the minister of finance, but getting agreement from the minister of finance was not easy.

I then asked for the concurrence of the vice ministers of both ministries. We managed to secure their agreement, and contacted the budget and tax authorities for a workable proposal. However, they were obstinate in their opposition to the idea, and we finally came up with a plan whereby the Korea Foreign Trade Association would collect a certain percentage of import prices once the government gave its permission that would be used for export promotion. On December 18, 1968, at the Export Promotion Expansion Meeting, President Park approved the following plan:

- Except for imports of raw materials for the manufacture of export products and for government use, the Korea Foreign Trade Association would collect an import surcharge as a special membership fee at the time of import approval or permission. [2]
- The special membership fee would begin at 1 percent of the import price, but would decrease as imports and the support system expanded.
- The special membership fee would be called the Export Promotion Special Account, and would be managed by a management com-

---

2. Only members of the Korea Foreign Trade Association can import. First of all, the members have to get import approval or permission from the banks that are acting for the government. Upon getting this approval, the member has to pay an import surcharge as a special membership fee of the association to the banks and the fee is credited to the association's account.

mittee that would be established at the Korea Foreign Trade Association.
- The use of the special account would be limited to export promotion activities after approval by the Export Promotion Expansion Meeting.
- The special membership fee would be collected starting in January 1969.

An extraordinary general assembly was held at the Korea Foreign Trade Association to vote on the Export Promotion Special Account. I attended the meeting, explained the importance of the new account, and asked the association to manage the fund carefully because in character it was no different from a tax on the population. By the end of the year the various acts had been revised to support the new account.

The focus of 1969, the year the account was introduced, was to give financial support to sales missions' overseas travels and to expand the Packaging and Design Center. In those days obtaining passports was difficult because of the acute shortage of foreign exchange, even when the purpose of travel was to promote Korean exports. As a result, Korean products lagged far behind their international counterparts in quality and design.

I believed more entrepreneurs should travel abroad to promote Korean products and to study foreign products to raise the standards of Korean goods. Back then Korean entrepreneurs took orders through the infrequent visits of foreign buyers or by letter. Thanks to the new account, traveling entrepreneurs could seek orders more aggressively, and many of them used their traveling expenses to buy samples. They also studied the markets they visited to improve their own products' marketability.

Packaging and design were also far below international standards. Products were not packaged using the materials and methods favored in international trade, so Korean products looked cheaper than they were and commanded lower prices. Facilities to produce packaging materials were imported so they could be produced domestically, and the materials that were hard to obtain were imported in large quantities for distribution at prices close to the original costs. To improve product design, commercial art specialists were trained and employed. In the end, design and packaging standards improved, helping Korean products to command prices that better reflected their value.

From the second year of the account, in addition to continued subsidies of the first year's projects, many projects were added: subsidies were given to help defray expenses incurred during trade activities by the Korea Trade Promotion Corporation and Korean embassy staff; an investment was made in the Koryo Trade Corporation, which handled small export orders; financial support was given to export examination institutes to obtain facilities and equipment; grants were given to the foreign language training center at the Hanguk University of Foreign Languages; support was given to projects that increased productivity; and grants were given to study countermeasures against possible import restrictions imposed by foreign countries.

The account also financed the construction of the twenty-two-story Trade Center Building in downtown Seoul and the purchase of the Korea Commercial Bank's government-owned stocks in a bid to establish a trade specialty bank in the future. It also financed the purchase of a lot in Samsong-dong south of the Han-gang River for the future construction of the Korea World Trade Center building. By the end of the 1980s a more comprehensive trade center building was needed and construction began on the Korea World Trade Center building once the old trade center and the commercial bank stocks had been sold.

The surcharge rate for the account has decreased with the steady increase in exports. It has been lowered six times, reaching 0.15 percent of import prices in 1990.

8

Chief of Staff to President Park Chung Hee: An Unexpected Appointment

On October 17, 1969, 65 percent of the voters in a national referendum approved a revision of the Korean Constitution that would allow the president to run for office three times. The Cabinet decided to resign to give the president a chance to begin afresh. I was relieved to have the opportunity to resign from my ministership without having committed major blunders, and began to bring home my belongings inconspicuously.

On October 20 the whole Cabinet resigned during the Cabinet meeting. Around three o'clock in the afternoon, my secretary rushed into my office and said that the president wanted to see me immediately. When I entered his office he was pacing back and forth in front of the window with his arms folded across his chest. He said he wanted to appoint me as chief of staff to the president and asked me to do my best.

I answered that I was not right for the position because although I knew a little about economics, I knew nothing about politics. He replied that economics was the very basis of governance. He then listed recent incidents of aggression by the Democratic People's Republic of Korea: the commando attack on the Blue House (the presidential residence) and the kidnapping of the American military vessel the Pueblo, both of which occurred in January 1968, and the downing of an American reconnaissance plane in April 1969. He stressed that unless we took effective measures, the situation would deteriorate, perhaps to the most perilous state since the Korean War. He revealed that he was not happy with the lukewarm American reaction to these events, and judging from Nixon's Guam Doctrine, which reflected American reluctance to become involved in Asia, he believed that the need to develop Korea's ability to defend itself was more pressing than ever. Because he had to occupy himself with national defense and diplomacy, he would like to leave me the task of dealing with the economy, which I should direct in cooperation with the economic ministers. He asked me to create good policies with an emphasis on export promotion and agricultural development, and brief him about them frequently. As I came out of the office after his fifty-minute monologue, I was overwhelmed by the role I had been given to play.

Freezing the Informal Money Market: The Emergency Decree for Economic Stability and Growth

The Korean economy grew at an unprecedented rate in the 1960s because of industrialization and the expansion of exports. However, in the second half of 1970, various unfavorable side effects of the spectacular growth brought about a recession. Most companies had a weak financial structure because they relied heavily on loans, especially from the informal money market, and repeated price hikes and depreciating foreign exchange rates adversely affected the economic environment.

The situation deteriorated as most industrial countries, the destinations of Korea's exports, also went into recession. The U.S. recession, which forced President Nixon to take emergency measures to defend the U.S. dollar in August 1971, especially affected the Korean business community. Economic growth declined from 13.8 percent in 1969 to 7.6 percent in 1970, 8.8 percent in 1971, and 5.7 percent in 1972. Many companies went bankrupt, which caused political and social unrest.

Historically speaking, the accumulation of domestic capital in Korea was meager. Before the liberation from Japan, the mainstay of capital had been land, with a sprinkling of funds from industrial and commercial entities, such as those involved in the textile, rubber, and brewery businesses and rice and flour mills. Consequently, after independence Korean enterprises needed to raise funds from the capital market to buy equipment. Unfortunately, the early stock market had only a distribution market and no issue market. To make matters worse, excessive speculation had brought about several national bond market and stock market crashes. As a result, the stock market was viewed with distrust. Enterprises could not obtain long-term funds for equipment by issuing stocks, and most entrepreneurs were seeped in the Confucian ideal of the family-centered business. Aside from pooled resources from within the family, they relied on domestic banks, foreign loans, and loans from the informal money market.

When a firm raises funds through stocks, recession can be overcome by paying smaller dividends. However, when a firm is heavily dependent on indirect financing, or indebtedness, the recession is harder to get out of because there is no alternative to paying fixed interest rates.

Moneylenders and the Threat of Withdrawing Loans

When the economy was experiencing stagnation, informal moneylenders were often very sensitive to rumors. If rumors were circulating that a particular large company was having a cash flow problem, moneylenders often decided to withdraw their loans simultaneously. Many companies went bankrupt when this happened.

The members of the Federation of Korean Industries were owners of large companies, but they were also experiencing a cash crunch and worrying about the possibility of private loans being withdrawn at short notice. Social unrest increased because when a large company went bankrupt, many small and medium-size companies that had dealings with it also went under. The federation had daily meetings and agreed that the emergency financial support measure that they had obtained with the cooperation of the banks and of government authorities was inadequate. It was time to get to the root of the problem. One day, the federation's chairman called on the president and asked for a solution. He explained that all companies were working hard, but that high interest loans from the informal money market were absorbing all their profits, and that they were all apprehensive because of the threat of moneylenders calling in their loans simultaneously. He said that the emergency loans from the banks were insufficient, and that many enterprises would go bankrupt if an emergency administrative measure concerning the informal money market loans were not introduced.

When the chairman left the president showed his concern about the collapse of the economy, and asked me what I thought of the chairman's suggestion. I asked the president to give me a night to mull over the matter, and told him that I would brief him the next morning.

Discussing my Proposal with the President

Naturally I could not sleep a wink thinking about possible countermeasures. The next morning, as soon as the president came down to his office, I briefed him on the following points:

- The crisis posed by business failures and bankruptcies resulted from the weak and unhealthy financial structure of Korean enterprises. Most of them relied on outside loans for about 80 percent of their funding, compared with an inside fundraising capacity of more than 50 percent for their counterparts in the industrial countries. The outside loans consisted not only of domestic and foreign loans, but also of informal money market funds that carried interest rates as high as 50 percent. The enterprises thus found a recession hard to survive because of the heavy burden of interest payments. On top of that, firms put short-term bank loans and high-interest informal money market funds into long-term finance for equipment. When private lenders decided to withdraw their money, the companies were left facing bankruptcy. As the chairman of the Federation of Korean Industries had said, the firms would lose ground irrespective of how hard they worked. If the situation were ignored, a chain reaction of business failures would result and a banking crisis could follow. The resultant bankruptcies and mass unemployment would hurt the national economy and Korean companies' credibility on the world credit market.
- The normal procedure would be to have the banks lend enterprises enough money to pay off their private loans. The Ministry of Finance estimated the volume of private loans held by Korean enterprises at W100 billion based on the amount of interest reported on income tax returns. The Federation of Korean Enterprises estimated the figure at W180 billion. However, the finance authority could only obtain W10 billion for a special support fund. Thus bank loans equivalent to the enterprises' private loans could not be obtained, and even if they could, the result would be inflation.

- The only way to decrease the rate of business failures, prevent a banking crisis, and avoid a chain reaction of bankruptcy and mass unemployment was to freeze the informal money market for a certain period of time. By activating the Presidential Emergency Decree spelled out in the Korean Constitution, all contracts between businesses and private moneylenders could be nullified and replaced by new contracts whereby the borrower would have a grace period and could repay the private loans in installments. Such loans would have a higher interest rate than that charged by public lending institutions, but much lower than their original rate. By transforming short-term, high interest loans into long-term, low interest loans, businesses' financial structure would improve and their profits would grow.
- When businesses were revived at the expense of private moneylenders, starting with the large corporations, they should be pressured to go public so as to increase their capital. Opening up family-owned companies to public shareholding would have many benefits. First, by promoting the issue market it would help resolve the shortage of capital within corporations. Second, management and ownership would be separated, with professional managers running the companies. Third, corporations' profits would be distributed to small shareholders, resulting in income redistribution. The gap between the rich and the poor would be narrowed, thereby contributing to the establishment of a stable society. Eventually such measures would compensate for the sacrifices made by small moneylenders as a result of the decree.
- To encourage the opening up of enterprises, the system of giving stock purchasing priority to employees, approved by legislation in 1968, could be actively promoted. Eventually employees could participate in the management of their companies, which would promote cooperation between labor and management.
- According to the Law Limiting the Earning of Interest, interest exceeding an annual rate of 36.5 percent was illegal, and those who earned above that rate were subject to punishment. Furthermore, most people earning interest from private loans were evading taxes. Most middle-class moneylenders were guilty on both counts, albeit unwittingly as concerned tax evasion, and it was regretful, but inevitable, that once the emergency decree took effect, the middle-class moneylenders would suffer along with the professional

sharks. To lessen the blow for the middle-class moneylenders, however, past violations of the law and tax evasion should not be investigated. The opening up of large companies should go hand-in-hand with the emergency decree to ensure success.

I enumerated the above points to the president, and added that such a measure was unprecedented. Although the work would be difficult, it could be done as long as the plan was kept secret during its preparation. Should the secret become public, the informal moneylenders would call in their loans from companies, causing an overnight, nationwide depression.

The Emergency Decree: Preparation and Content

The president grasped the gist of my briefing and made an immediate decision. He assured me that opening the enterprises would follow the emergency decree so as to reap the resultant social and economic benefits. He asked me how the practical preparation was to be launched, and I answered that forming a small, elite task force headed by Blue House aide Kim Yong-hwan would be the best way.

The preparation was finished by the end of June 1972, and the decree was to take effect on July 1. However, the announcement had to be postponed until August 3, because the North-South Regulation Committee, the first joint committee discussing the reunification of Korea, decided to make a historic announcement on July 4.

On August 3, 1972, the president announced the President's Emergency Decree for Economic Stability and Growth, an unprecedented move in a free economy. The central point of the decree was that all credits and liabilities between businesses and private moneylenders were immediately nullified and replaced with new contracts.

Under the new contracts, borrowers had a three-year grace period and could repay the loans in installments over a five-year period at a 1.35 percent monthly interest rate (16.20 percent per year). If the lenders wished, the loans could be diverted to equity shares. According to a Bank of Korea survey, the weighted average monthly interest for private loans was 3.84 percent. Thus the interest payment had been cut by one-third. No accurate data about the total size of the informal money market existed. To everybody's surprise, the reported loans amounted to W345.6 billion, almost 80 percent of the currency in circulation. Thanks to the decree, a domino effect of business failures and a banking crisis were averted, and the growth rate, which had dropped to 7.8 percent by the early 1970s, soared to 14.1 percent in 1973.

The main points of the President's Emergency Decree for Economic Stability and Growth were as follows:

- Private loans held by enterprises as of August 2, 1972, had to be reported by August 9.
- Financial institutions would issue special bonds totaling W200 billion, from which the enterprises would be provided with long-term, low interest loans to pay off 30 percent of their total short-term bank loans. Loan payments were to be deposited in the Bank of Korea to prevent the currency in circulation from increasing.
- The government would invest W1 billion in the Small and Medium-Size Enterprises Credit Guarantee Fund and the Agriculture, Forestry, and Fishery People's Credit Guarantee Fund. In addition, to reinforce the credit guarantee system, all banking institutions would establish credit guarantee funds by setting aside 0.5 percent of the total loans for five years.
- An industrial rationalization fund of W50 billion would be established at the Korea Development Bank to supply long-term, low interest loans to support mergers and the modernization of priority industries to improve their efficiency, profitability, and competitiveness. Firms meeting the rationalization standards defined by the Industry Rationalization Deliberation Committee could apply for these loans. In addition, the depreciation premium rate for the investment in fixed equipment by major industries would be raised from 30 percent to 40 to 80 percent, and the investment deduction rate for corporation tax and income tax would be raised from 6 percent to 10 percent.
- To relax the rigid government budget allocation practices, the fixed ratios of grants to local government bodies would be abolished.

Upon issuing the decree, the president directed the Cabinet to implement the following measures:

- Lower dramatically the interest rate charged by financial institutions
- Stabilize the exchange rate at W500 to the U.S. dollar
- Keep utility rates constant

- Freeze price increases at an annual rate of 3 percent
- Restrict the size of 1973 budgets.

Results of the Emergency Decree

The decree had three immediate results. First, a total of W345.6 billion in private loans, equivalent to 42 percent of total bank loans, was controlled by a 16.2 percent annual interest rate compared to the previous rate of up to 50 percent. Second, the government invested W200 billion to convert part of the banks' short-term, high interest loans to long-term, low interest loans (8 percent annual interest rate). Third, the government supplied W50 billion to establish a fund for industrial rationalization. Firms that met the rationalization criteria could apply for long-term, low interest loans.

To help reduce the burden of enterprises' interest payments and to promote private investment, the government lowered the banks' regular deposit interest rate from 17.4 to 12.6 percent and the interest rate on general loans from 19.0 to 15.5 percent. This also reduced enterprises' production costs.

The excessive indebtedness of Korean enterprises was one of their most prominent weaknesses. It lowered their profits, raised consumer prices, and compromised their competitiveness on the world market. The ratio of the manufacturing industry's financial expenses to sales rose to 9.18 percent in 1971, but the Emergency Decree brought the figure down to 7.08 percent in 1972, close to the 1969 level. In June 1973 the figure fell further to 5.69 percent. These figures eloquently demonstrate the decree's success. As a result, the international competitive edge of Korean companies improved dramatically.

Coincidentally, the international business environment also became favorable for Korea. With the devaluation of the U.S. dollar in December 1971, followed by Nixon's introduction of dollar defense measures in August, the currencies of the Federal Republic of Germany, France, Italy, Japan, and the United Kingdom appreciated, with increases ranging from 7.57 percent to 16.88 percent. From July 1972 to June 1973 Korean exports increased by 75.6 percent compared with July 1971 to June 1972, and the first half of 1973 showed a 91.0 percent increase in exports compared with the same period the previous year. Although imports also increased after the emergency decree, the first half of 1973 showed a surplus balance of payments of US$124 million, a remarkable turnaround from the early 1972 deficit.

Following the decree the manufacturing industry grew 30.8 percent in the first quarter of 1973 compared to the same period in 1972 (when it grew 13.2 percent), and domestic fixed investment increased 16.2 percent (a decrease of 7.8 percent). All in all, the GNP of the first quarter of 1973 increased 19.0 percent compared to the first quarter of 1972.

The Emergency Decree not only brought the struggling economy back on the fast development track, but it also established solid ground for continued economic development in the 1970s. Thanks to the emergency measure, Korea could later weather the oil crises of 1973 and 1978.

The Law on Facilitating the Opening of Closed Corporations

When the emergency decree had been successfully completed, the minister of finance (Nam Duck-woo) hurried to draft the Law on Facilitating the Opening of Closed Corporations. The law passed the National Assembly at the end of 1972 and came into effect in January 1973. Its purpose was to stimulate the improvement of corporations' financial structure and to induce the fund supply system to rely on stock issues.

According to the new law, the government could order the opening up of corporations, and if they did not comply, the government could wield strong disciplinary measures, such as levying unfavorable taxes and limiting banking support.

In early 1973, when the Deliberation Committee for Opening Corporations was inaugurated, many corporations voluntarily went public. However, some family-oriented conglomerates and large corporations were reluctant to open up now that their financial crisis was over. On May 1974 the president issued special instructions to the Cabinet, pointed out that some entrepreneurs' were using outdated management methods, and called for an opening of closed corporations. These instructions also forced entrepreneurs to dispose of large real estate holdings and inessential affiliates.

The measures were vigorously carried out until the president's assassination in 1979. From 1956, the year the stock exchange opened, to 1972, the year before the introduction of the Law on Facilitating the Opening of Closed Corporations, only 66 firms had gone public, but during 1973–79, more than 300 companies went public. If the next administration had followed the same policy, the country's economic power would not be as concentrated as it is now.

With the new law, the issue market of the stock exchange became active and corporation bonds appeared on the scene. Until the end of 1971 corporation bonds were unheard of on the Korean stock market. Now corporation bonds were issued and spread rapidly, emerging as a stable source of companies' long-term investment funds. The value of corporation bonds reached W300 billion in 1975 and W600 billion in 1979. In 1980 the total issue of stocks and corporation bonds exceeded W1 trillion.

Introduction of the Value Added Tax

In October 1969, when I became chief of staff to the president, one of my major policy recommendations was that the minister of finance remain in his position long enough to reform the tax system with a long-term view.

The Background to Tax Reform

My proposal was accepted, so for the next ten years Korea had only two ministers of finance. From 1948 to 1969 the average minister of finance stayed in the job for only eleven months, far too short a time to work on a comprehensive tax system. Since 1948 the Ministry of Finance had revised the tax system every year, including some major reforms, such as the overall reform in 1949, the temporary wartime reform during the Korean War, and the postwar reform of 1954. In 1959 the government announced the Three-Year Economic Revival Plan, and to support the plan prepared to revise the tax system. Twenty-two tax laws were to be changed, five of which were revised in 1959 and the rest in 1960. In 1967 another tax reform supported the Five-Year Economic Development Plan.

In addition, small-scale tax revisions took place every year, partly to solve problems emerging from changing economic conditions and tax administration, and partly to secure revenues for the national budget. As of 1969, the Korean tax system had a strong tendency to serve as a revenue collector without paying due consideration to the imbalance of the tax burdens among the different classes. Because of the efforts over the years to increase tax revenues through frequent, partial revisions, the system had become extremely complicated. Also, because the system centered on the high direct tax, various conflicts arose in the process of operation. Levying taxes on administratively assessed incomes resulted in tax evasion and corruption and the indirect tax system had still not been modernized. Indirect taxes fell into eight categories: business tax, commodity tax, textile tax, petroleum products tax, admission tax, travel tax, gas and electricity tax, and entertainment and food tax. Each of the indirect taxes had its own rate structure as well as a different tax base and administrative procedure. Introducing a simple, low indirect tax that would generate high revenues to compensate for the gap expected when the high income tax was relaxed and the tax burden was reduced for those in the low-income bracket was deemed urgent.

In 1971 the Ministry of Finance announced changes to the long-term tax system, which included an overall composite income tax and the introduction of a value added tax (VAT) in the foreseeable future. By 1976 the tax burden on the low-income bracket was to be reduced, and to correct the imbalance in tax burdens among classes, the composite income tax was to be introduced in the direct tax system and the VAT in the indirect tax system. In 1967 the European Economic Community agreed to introduce a VAT that was to be in effect in all member countries by 1971. France was the first to inaugurate the VAT in 1968, and Italy was the last to introduce it in 1973. Even the United Kingdom instituted the VAT to be eligible to join the Community. The government authorities and tax experts around the world had a keen interest in the VAT.

The VAT is an indirect tax, a kind of general consumption tax. Generally speaking, in the beginning stage of economic development, tariffs in the indirect tax category are dominant, but with the development of domestic industry, revenues from tariffs decrease, whereas the individual consumption taxes increase. Before the development of Korea's domestic industry, the individual consumption tax was limited to such items as liquor, tobacco, automobiles, and fuel. The individual consumption tax was easy to operate and could generate a considerable amount of revenue. However, with the development of domestic production, the number of taxable items increased, which complicated the system. When a new product was made, it could not be taxed until the tax law was revised to include it on the list of taxable items. In other words, the government taxed every item separately. In terms of the individual consumer tax, the ability to tax individuals based on their ability to pay was diminished as more varied consumption patterns developed. Therefore, as the economic structure became more highly developed, a general consumption tax on a variety of items was deemed more desirable in relation to tax payments, administration, and fairness.

Under the general consumption tax, the number of taxable items can be increased and administration is easier as long as a single tax rate structure is in effect. Use of a single tax rate structure avoids discriminatory taxing and can achieve neutrality. An exception can be made by taxing luxury items heavily.

As Carl Shoup, the tax expert who recommended tax reform—including the introduction of a VAT—in Japan after the World War II, pointed out, the VAT is the "newest form of the consumption tax in its developmental stage, and perhaps the last-stage general consumption tax."

I Support the VAT

When the minister of finance consulted me before announcing the changes to the long-term tax system, I wholeheartedly agreed with the idea of a VAT and pledged my full cooperation. I had already received suggestions from prominent economists about the merits of introducing a VAT.

The VAT exists in many forms, but the one Korea adopted was the same type the European Economic Community had employed. It is a tax levied at all stages of the production and distribution of goods and services on the value the entrepreneur or business adds at each step of transaction. In other words, it is a tax levied on the added value by subtracting the purchase price from the sales price, unlike the business tax or the commodity tax, which is based on the total sales figure. The VAT is different from the commodity tax in that all goods and services are taxed at all stages of the transaction unless they are exempted from the tax by law, whereas the commodity tax is applied to only a certain stage of the transaction. However, as concerns a VAT, the taxed portion is not taxed again, so consumers do not pay a cumulative tax. For taxpayers the effect is the same as paying a sales tax at the retail level.

The VAT is calculated by deducting the tax paid on the purchase price from the sales tax on the goods and services supplied. Thus business people ask those at the previous stage of production to issue a tax or sales invoice. The taxation at the importation level serves as a basis for the tax base at the manufacturing level and so forth through manufacturing, wholesale, retail, and so on. A system of tax invoices permits the collection of tax information on all those involved, and mutual audits are possible, preventing tax evasion and promoting taxation based on evidence.

I supported the VAT because many taxpayers complained about taxation based on estimation, and people viewed enterprises with suspicion because they believed their owners were becoming rich by evading taxes. I believed that by solving such problems, the financial situation would improve, social justice could be practiced, and society could become more harmonious and stable.

Implementation of the Proposed Tax Reform

On July 1, 1977, six years after the announcement of the reform of long-term taxes, the VAT was implemented. During the tax reform of 1971, the categories of business tax were simplified from twenty to eleven and the number of tax rates was reduced from twenty-three to sixteen. In addition, taxes were raised an average of 18.7 percent. These revisions were preparatory steps for the introduction of a general consumer tax, such as a sales tax or a VAT.

At this point the Ministry of Finance invited international VAT experts to study the possibility of introducing such a tax in Korea. In 1972 James D. Daignan, the Irish tax expert who was in charge of introducing the VAT in Ireland, arrived, followed in 1973 by Shoup. In 1974 preparations began in earnest.

In July 1974 a Korean delegation was sent to Belgium, the European Economic Community, the Federal Republic of Germany, Japan, Taiwan (China), and the United Kingdom to study the introduction, implementation, and outcome of a VAT. In 1975 the director general of the Tax Bureau was dispatched to the United Kingdom for a thorough study of the British system. In 1975 and 1976 Alan Tait, the International Monetary Fund's tax expert, was invited to review the VAT's effects on prices and income distribution. Daignan was invited again in 1976 and served as a consultant during the drafting of the legislation and the setting up of the administration of the VAT.

According to Daignan's report, the business tax, the commodity tax, and the textile tax (the major taxes in the indirect tax system) could be replaced by a 10 percent VAT, and a special consumption tax could be levied on luxury items such as automobiles, televisions, and air conditioners. On its return from Europe, the Korean VAT delegation suggested a single-rate, consumption-type VAT that could be practiced by deducting the tax levied on the previous level of production or distribution. These recommendations became the basis of the legislation.

The Tait reports of 1975 contained two main recommendations concerning the introduction of the VAT. First, a 10 percent VAT would be sufficient to replace all the business and commodity taxes. Second, existing business and commodity taxes ranged from 0.5 percent to 300 percent. If they were all converted to a 10 percent VAT, there would be a dramatic increase in the middle-class's consumption of luxury items and durable consumer goods that were formerly taxed at considerably higher rates. Therefore, levying a special consumption tax on these items would be desirable.

As for the review of the tax rate and the VAT's effect on prices, the Tait report of 1976 commented that considering the expected revenue increase following the introduction of the VAT, a tax rate of 10 percent would be sufficient. As for the VAT's effect on prices, Korean entrepreneurs who had experienced both continuous inflation and economic development might raise prices using the VAT as an excuse if a price-raising element existed, but might not lower prices fully if a price-lowering element existed. Therefore, the government needed to supervise and regulate prices with great care. If government supervision were successful, price changes would be limited to a range of plus or minus 1 percent.

In April 1975 the Tax Deliberation Committee was established, and the draft of the VAT was published in January 1976. During the deliberation process heated arguments erupted. The negative arguments centered around three points: (a) Korea was not ready for a VAT because the business community did not keep reliable records, (b) it would have a significant effect on prices, and (c) it is a regressive tax.

The National Assembly Approves the Proposal

The National Assembly finally approved the VAT in November, and it was promulgated on December 22, 1976, to take effect on July 1, 1977.

On completion of the legislation, the Office of National Tax Administration (ONTA) launched active preparation activities for the six months prior to the law taking effect. The preparations included educating tax administrators and launching publicity campaigns to inform taxpayers about the changes in the tax laws. Three nationwide practice sessions on filling the new tax returns were held in which 830,000 taxpayers participated. To encourage the exchange of tax invoices, tax incentives were offered to those businesses that installed cash registers. To minimize the number of cases where an anticipated reduction in prices did not occur or an unexpected price increase took place, the ONTA prepared item-by-item information about the price increase rates and margin rates for all stages of transactions, and store owners were obligated to display this information in their stores.

Opposition to the Immediate Introduction of the VAT

The last step in the preparation period was to have businesses re-register with their local tax offices between May 10 and June 10, 1977. Around the end of May, some working-level government officials in charge of price policies began to argue that implementation of the VAT should be postponed because prices might soar. They based their claim on that part of the VAT law that specified that when the economic situation made it advisable, the president could postpone the implementation of the VAT.

When such views were voiced inside the administration, some ruling party and opposition assemblymen, pressured by the industrial and commercial sectors of their constituencies, began to push for postponement. Major business associations climbed aboard the bandwagon. They claimed that the VAT would cause price increases beyond the 10 percent limit, and that exchanging tax invoices was unreasonable because record keeping was not an everyday practice in Korea. They insisted that even if the VAT were implemented, the rate should be lower than the planned basic rate of 13 percent to minimize its impact on prices.

During the first half of 1977 exports had increased steadily, exceeding the rate of increase in imports, and the balance of invisible trade showed steady growth thanks to the income generated by construction sites in the Middle East. As a result, the balance of payments showed a surplus of US$950 million, which increased the amount of currency in circulation enormously. The government made all-out efforts to constrain liquidity by raising the reserve requirements for deposits in May, suppressing the importation of short-term foreign loans and trade credit in August, and depositing the remittances from overseas construction in special accounts in October.

Aside from the currency problem, changes in the weather and the economic environment had conspired to raise the prices of meat, fish, vegetables, and fruit. Wholesale food prices in the first half of 1977 jumped 10.5 percent compared to the same period in 1976, and the prices of nonfood goods rose 3.6 percent. The trend seemed likely to continue for some time.

Explaining the Rationale and the President Agrees

The arguments supporting a delay in the implementation of the VAT surfaced because of such price trends. In Cabinet meetings, the postponement of the VAT was repeatedly discussed without arriving at a conclusion. On June 13, the president convened a meeting in the Blue House. He asked one participant after another how they felt about the implementation of the VAT. Most were in favor of postponement, and a consensus favoring that position seemed to be gaining momentum. Toward the end of the debates I stated the following opinion:

"Under the VAT system, agricultural and fishing products are exempt from taxation because they are essentials. Therefore farmers and fishermen won't be affected. Also the smallest merchants and industrialists (those not required to have business licenses because their taxable earnings are negligible) are excluded from having to pay the VAT. Among the remaining 830,000 merchants and industrialists, those whose annual sales are less than W12 million will not be subject to the VAT because they lack the requisite record keeping ability. Instead they will pay a simple 2 percent tax that is similar to the old one. Almost 670,000 people, 80.9 percent of the 830,000 merchants and industrialists, fall in this category. Thus, only 160,000 business will have to follow the new tax law by exchanging tax invoices and keeping records. Of these, 20,000 are corporations that already have the necessary accounting structure, and the rest can keep records and exchange tax invoices because they already have cashiers or treasurers. Also there is a simple way of using a receipt as a tax invoice.

"A certain economic sector argues that the VAT should be postponed because exchanging tax invoices is unreasonable in a situation where record keeping is not common. However, such a claim is not valid because receipts can replace tax invoices as I mentioned before. Also the VAT is a consumer tax, one of the indirect taxes like the existing business tax and the commodity tax. The tax is included in the sales price and transferred to the consumer. The VAT taxpayer is the consumer, not the business. Therefore those favoring postponement reflect a fear that evading taxes, which was possible to do in the past, will become more difficult. In the existing system, the exact transaction amount is hard to pinpoint and taxing on administratively estimated profits is practiced, resulting in a loss in tax revenue caused by the difference between real earnings and the tax base. Furthermore, because the business tax base becomes the base for the individual business income tax or the corporation tax, the amount of taxes paid by businesses has been automatically reduced. The complaint about the VAT comes from the 160,000 people who don't like the way the new tax prevents the evasion of income or corporation taxes.

"The VAT is not a new tax levied on the people. It just forces enterprises to pay the government the tax that consumers pay them. The new tax will help collect the portion of the income and corporation tax that has been evaded. The prevention of the tax evasion will naturally increase tax revenue, but more important, the people's suspicions that enterprises are tax evaders will diminish. The change in perception is important for the stability of our society. VAT revenues will increase in line with economic development. When the financial source of economic development is secured, the high direct tax system can be reformed to be more lenient. Eventually, the increasing revenue from the VAT will satisfy the increasing demand for social welfare funds needed to assist the poor and the elderly. Of course, it will take time before the VAT works smoothly, and there will be unexpected problems to be solved along the way. Also the VAT has an inherent element of price instability. However, the VAT will make the tax and financial revenues healthy and its positive aspects far outweigh the danger of price hikes exceeding the mandated 10 percent level. During the first half of 1977, the prices of agricultural and fish products (those exempt from the VAT) soared, but industrial products remained stable.

"Even if the VAT increases the prices of industrial products, the overall price of wholesale products will rise less than 15 percent a year, and even that will be limited to the first year of the VAT's implementation. The VAT has been legislated after six years of careful study by domestic and foreign experts, and it is about to take effect. The public has been educated and there have been three filing rehearsals for all enterprises. The price stability guideline for each industrial product has been prepared and countermeasures have been considered. It is the first time in Korean tax reform history that such careful preparation was done. If it is delayed this time, it can't be tried again until 1980 because of the upcoming election for the National Assembly in 1978. By that time, the revolt by the business sector will be greater because it was postponed once. Despite expected problems, it is best to go ahead with the plan. As for the tax rate, the basic rate is set at 13 percent plus or minus 3 percent, but in view of the threat of price increases and widespread anxiety, it would be best to apply a 10 percent elastic tax rate from the very beginning."

After my long speech the president decided to push for the original plan, except for a change of the rate to 10 percent. He directed the relevant ministries to cooperate so that the VAT could be implemented smoothly and to prevent price hikes.

The Process and Effects of the VAT

When the VAT took effect on July 1, 1977, the ONTA organized an inspection to see whether or not the government-set prices for 795 products were being observed. Also the items excluded from the government list had administrative guidance prices. Thanks to inspections and guidance by the ONTA as well as cooperation by the merchants, prices did not rise as much as many people had feared. In 1977, the annual wholesale price increased 10.1 percent (a 21.1 percent increase in food prices and a 5.4 percent increase in nonfood prices). Consumer prices rose 10.9 percent (a 12.3 percent increase in food prices and a 9.0 percent increase in nonfood prices).

In the second half of 1977, after the implementation of the VAT, wholesale prices increased 4.1 percent and consumer prices increased 3.9 percent. These increases were due to a hike in food prices that had nothing to do with the VAT. It was attributable to a combination of factors: a small harvest of greenhouse-grown crops caused by unexpected cold weather in January and February, a slump in fishing, and a dramatic increase in the demand for meat fueled by increased incomes. However, the prices of industrial products and services remained stable. It is true that there was confusion in the beginning until prices stabilized at the new level, and that merchants were unhappy during the price supervision period. Yet prices became stable in two months and did not exceed 10 percent. From the second year of implementation, the VAT did not affect prices.

Another question raised during the introduction of the new tax was whether or not taxpayers could adapt to the complicated new system despite the three filing rehearsals and the ONTA's education efforts. The filing of tax returns during the first six months, which consisted of two estimated filings and one confirmed filing, showed that 99 percent of taxpayers had participated. The majority of taxpayers who had to give tax invoices also did so: 71.3 percent in the first six months of 1977, improving to 83.8 percent during 1978–82.

Indirect taxes accounted for 56.2 percent of total tax revenues in 1976, but from 1978 they consistently accounted for more than 60 percent. VAT revenues reflected economic development: in 1978 they amounted to W830 billion, but by 1986 they had risen to more than W3 trillion, 38.7 percent of total domestic tax revenues.

The Urgent Need for National Security and Industrial Policies

In his 1970 New Year's address President Park announced that the year's goal was: "To build on the one hand and to defend the country on the other," the same as the goal for the previous two years.

The Korean peninsula had been under a cease-fire since 1953, but the Democratic People's Republic of Korea (North Korea) was trying to reunite the two Koreas by force, and numerous infiltration and provocation attempts had taken place. In the late 1960s and the early 1970s, such incidents increased in number and intensity. In 1968, the Blue House was attacked by North Korean commandos; the American reconnaissance ship the Pueblo was kidnapped; and more than 100 North Korean commandos sneaked into the eastern mountains, attacking nearby villages intermittently for more than a month. In 1969 North Koreans shot down an American aircraft, and on Memorial Day they bombed the National Cemetery in an attempt to assassinate the president. On three occasions in 1970, armed spies and vessels landed on the east coast. In July 1970, despite the increasing tension, the U.S. government decided to withdraw one American infantry division stationed in Korea as dictated by the Nixon Doctrine.

In response to such developments, in 1968 President Park organized 2.5 million people as army reserves, and in 1970 he directed the minister of the Economic Planning Board to build factories for producing conventional weapons. The Economic Planning Board devised a plan in which four factories, including a heavy machinery factory, were to be built with foreign loans. In November 1971, during a briefing, the president was informed that the efforts to negotiate loans with Japan, the United States, and various European countries had failed. On his way to the Blue House the president expressed his disappointment, and I decided to get involved in the construction of a defense industry.

I was deep in thought when I received a telephone call from Oh Won-chul, an assistant vice minister in the Ministry of Commerce and Industry, who had been present at the briefing. He said that he had an idea of how to build up the defense industry. I immediately summoned him to my office and listened to this excellent technocrat's idea.

A Proposal for Building Up the Defense Industry

After intense discussion Oh Won-chul and I agreed on the following points:

- The Ministry of Defense was pushing for the government to construct factories to produce weapons, but except for the M16 automatic rifle factory that was already under construction, such factories were better left unbuilt as they were economically infeasible because of fluctuations in demand. Taiwan's (China) and Japan's systems before and during World War II both provided examples of the kinds of problems that could be incurred. There was also the challenge of attracting first-rate engineers and skilled workers away from the private sector.
- Private armaments factories are economically infeasible because expensive, specialized machines must stay idle when the demand is low.
- All weapons can be dissembled into parts. Well-designed parts could be manufactured in different factories and eventually assembled to make precise weapons.
- Modern weapons required the same manufacturing standards as sophisticated heavy and chemical industries. For the Korean economy, the promotion of the heavy and chemical industries was essential, not only out of economic necessity, but also for national security reasons.
- The promotion of the Korean defense industry should be pursued in line with the build up of the heavy and chemical industries. Each factory could specialize in a particular weapon part to minimize economic loss.
- Although the construction of weapons production facilities was the fundamental issue, securing and training engineers and skilled workers was just as important.

After the discussion I took Oh to the president's office. The president showed a great deal of interest in our ideas and asked various questions for three or four hours. He then agreed in principle; however, he did not like the fact that munitions could not be produced for some four or five years because the heavy and chemical industries had to be built first. Considering the North's behavior and the American military reduction plan, he strongly hoped that weapons could be produced within two or three years.

I argued that specific weapons factories could be built in two or three years, but that promoting the defense industry as part of the heavy and chemical industries would require at least four or five years. I emphasized that in case of emergency, private capacity could quickly be converted to defense needs to mass produce weapons. The president pondered for a long time, and then agreed that the heavy and chemical industries could be built simultaneously with the defense industry, and that production capacity could be maximized in emergency situations. He instructed us to start to work in cooperation with the pertinent ministries. He soon called back again, however, and said that he himself would be in charge of the heavy and chemical industries and the defense industry and that he wanted to move Oh to the Blue House as his personal advisor. I suggested that he create a Second Economic Staff Office and appoint Oh as a senior secretary at the rank of vice minister. The next day, Oh was awarded such a post.

The Plan to Promote the Heavy and Chemical Industries

During his 1973 New Year's address the president revealed that the government would promote the heavy and chemical industries so that by 1980 Korea could be one of the leading developing countries, with a per capita GNP of US$1,000 and exports of US$10 billion.

The government selected six fields for a concerted effort: iron and steel, nonferrous metals, machinery, shipbuilding, electronics, and chemicals. The Heavy and Chemical Industries Promotion Act was enacted to support these industries by providing tax and banking incentives and exempting young engineers and skilled workers from compulsory military service.

The development strategies were as follows:

- To promote economic feasibility and competitiveness, the factories' sizes would be on a par with international standards.
- The domestic market was too small for these large factories. Therefore, the heavy and chemical industries would be promoted as strategic export industries in an attempt to practice economics of scale.
- To promote and secure engineers and skilled workers, the education and training systems would be overhauled. A skills licensing system would be introduced, and every Korean would be encouraged to possess at least one skill.
- Five strategic industrial research institutes in the fields of shipbuilding, machinery, petrochemicals, electronics, and marine science would be established to support the technological aspects of the plan.
- The industries would be located in purpose—built because (a) the heavy and chemical industries have strong forward and backward linkages among themselves; (b) they require large-scale social overhead capital for water, electricity, and transportation; and (c) some of the factories produce a great deal of pollution.

In 1974, with the cooperation of the financial institutions the government established the National Investment Fund (NIF) to facilitate the financing of long-term investment in plants and equipment for the heavy and chemical industries. The sources of the NIF's funds included contributions by banks and insurance companies, and public funds such as the civil servants' pension fund and the veteran's pension fund. The NIF mobilized the necessary funds from these sources by receiving deposits or issuing national investment bonds. In addition, the Industrial Parks Development Promotion Law was enacted and the Industrial Parks Development Corporation was founded to oversee the construction of six industrial parks.

The Heavy and Chemicals Industry Strategy in Retrospect

Korea had achieved a sort of miracle by developing a full set of industries—light industry, heavy and chemicals industries (HCI), and a defense industry—since 1962, the year light industry took off. After the assassination of President Park, criticism surfaced that excessive investment in HCI had aggravated inflation and that excessive facilities caused the misallocation of resources. However, I had pushed for the defense industry despite the expected inflation because of the imminent American military withdrawal. When I had been the director general of finance in 1959, I had the experience of reducing a 30 percent inflation rate to 2 to 3 percent by instituting a financial stabilization program. I was confident that once the HCI and defense industry were completed we could curb inflation with a strong financial stabilization program. President Park agreed with me. We were proven right when the next administration successfully curbed inflation in the early 1980s.

In general, large-scale factories built with an eye to the next ten to twenty years tend to face temporary idleness. As for the overinvestment in HCI, the government had planned to export HCI products as vigorously as Japan did in the 1950s and the 1960s. Unfortunately, the key officials in charge of HCI were dismissed in the next administration, and these efforts were abandoned. However, I have no doubt that the promotion of HCI in the 1970s was the driving force behind the rapid growth and large surplus in current accounts of the latter half of the 1980s.

9

Helping the President with His Strategic Projects

As chief of staff to the president I performed two functions, one was to make policy proposals, at the instance of the president, in areas of my expertise and competence, and the other was to help the president implement his brilliant, innovative, and fruitful ideas about development strategy. The previous chapter has already described my role in policymaking. This chapter will cover my other duty and describe how I helped the president implement three major initiatives.

I assisted the President in implementing the following projects, creatively conceived by him.

The *Saemaul* Movement

Coming from a farming family, during his eighteen years in office President Park was obsessed with improving the plight of farmers. When he grabbed power by means of the coup, his Revolution Pledge included the phrase: "To quickly solve the problem of people struggling with starvation and despair." On May 25, 1961, only nine days after the coup, he took a measure to eliminate high interest loans to farmers. On June 11, he initiated the National Reconstruction Movement for encouraging the people to become independent, but to work together. Both measures had only limited success because of the shortage of resources.

He soon realized that the key to agricultural reform lay in improving the soil, developing water resources for irrigation, introducing protection measures against floods and droughts, reorganizing farmland for mechanized farming, diversifying crops, developing livestock, and instigating price support policies for rice and barley. On all these fronts he took prompt and effective action. However, the most brilliant and original project that he conceived for rural development was the *Saemaul* (or New Village) Movement.

The Birth of the Saemaul Movement

In July 1969 heavy rainstorms hit southeastern Korea. On August 4, 1969, the president stopped at a village during his tour of the disaster area and saw that not only had the damage been cleaned up, but that the village's roads had been expanded and the houses' roofs and walls were better constructed than was usual. When he showed his curiosity, the villagers told him that they had decided to restore and improve their village by volunteering their time and labor. On his way back to Seoul, the president thought up a plan that would awaken farmers' spirit of industriousness and encourage self-help and cooperation.

In April 1970, during the provincial governors meeting, the president expressed his belief that if the farmers did not have the will and desire to improve themselves, their poverty would continue forever. He directed government officials and farmers to work together by launching the *Saemaul* Movement.

The Ministry of Home Affairs drew up a plan for the *Saemaul* Movement and designed a training program for *Saemaul* leaders, both men and women. Training programs for regional and central government officials followed shortly thereafter. In 1974 Cabinet-level officials participated in the program, and later college professors, journalists, entrepreneurs, artists, and religious leaders received the *Saemaul* education.

The Movement Gains Momentum

The movement's scope in the first few months was limited. However, it soon got an impetus from a development in the cement industry, which was having a surplus cement problem. This unexpectedly provided an opportunity to develop a mechanism for the rapid spread of the movement. A great example of how a problem in one area can become a blessing in another!

One summer day, a prominent ruling party member paid a visit to the Blue House to discuss party matters. Afterwards he mentioned the difficulties the Korean cement industry was facing because of surplus production and asked the president for special financial assistance. The president directed me to find a way to funnel the surplus cement into the *Saemaul* Movement.

The minister and I studied the budget of the Ministry of Home Affairs, but the ministry clearly could not afford to buy the surplus cement. I contacted the deputy prime minister and he said that if it had to be done, he could somehow come up with W3 billion. The next day the president summoned the deputy prime minister and the minister of home affairs for a long discussion and decided to use the W3 billion to buy the cement and put it in the *Saemaul* Movement.

In October 1970 some 300 to 350 bags of cement were distributed free of charge to each of 34,665 rural villages on the condition that they be used for communal projects. Regional administrative offices demonstrated examples of improvement projects that villagers could choose from, which included expanding the road leading to the village, building a small bridge, roofing, improving a well, strengthening a river bank, or building a communal bath house. The decision about what project to undertake was left to the villagers. The average village had 80 households, which meant that 300 cement bags amounted to 4 bags per household. In other words, the government's financial support for each household was about W4,000 (US$12.61).

The villagers' response during the first year of the project (November 1970–March 1971) appeared more positive than the government had expected. In many cases villagers also contributed some of their own money to projects as well as providing an enormous amount of labor to accomplish elaborate communal projects. According to a thorough government evaluation, 16,000 out of almost 35,000 villages achieved something worthwhile.

Emphasis on Self-Help and Cooperation

In 1972, the second year of the *Saemaul* Movement, President Park decided to support only the successful villages by providing 500 cement bags and 1-ton iron bars. The Ministry of Home Affairs expressed dismay and the ruling party was shocked, saying that excluded villagers might not support the ruling party at the next election. However, the president believed in supporting those villages that helped themselves.

During a government-party joint meeting at the Blue House, he forcefully expressed his support for the principle of rewarding those that deserved rewards and punishing those that deserved punishment, saying that he would gladly step down if he lost the election because of that. I was also anxious that if the villages that did not make the list were left out every year, it could pose a political problem. However, the villagers responded in a surprising manner. Out of the villages that did not make the list 6,108, or one-third, made their own efforts to participate in the *Saemaul* Movement. These villagers did not complain, but vowed that they would do better in the future.

Under the principle of giving priority to successful villages, the villages were classified into three categories: basic, self-help, and independent villages (the independent villages being the most successful). Material support was given only to the self-help and independent villages. The basic villages became embarrassed as their neighboring villages transformed themselves. Farmers were caught up in the spirit of competition and cooperation and spread the *Saemaul* Movement across the country. Because the villagers were intent on obtaining government support, the basic villages soon became self-help villages and the self-help villages were promoted to independent villages.

From 1974 rural incomes rose to the level earned by urban laborers, and the goal for 1981 was achieved ahead of schedule in 1977. By that time 98 percent of the villages had became independent villages and no basic villages remained.

Insulation from Politics

In addition to the principle of rewarding those that deserved rewards and punishing those that deserved punishment, the president ensured that political elements did not creep into the movement. In the early 1970s the ruling party discussed the possibility of inviting the *Saemaul* leaders to join the ruling party. When the president heard about it, his face registered the most displeased expression I had ever seen. He said, "Nobody can use the *Saemaul* Movement for political purposes. The movement should transcend politics and remain a pure people's movement in order to move on. If a party member was chosen as a *Saemaul* leader, we can't ask him to leave the party, but no leader should be invited to join the party." He ordered his staff to observe whether or not his policy was being carried out.

It was natural for every village to have a dissenting element, albeit to different degrees. If villagers sensed that they were being used for political ends, the *Saemaul* Movement would not have been such a success. I can state with confidence that it was a success because all villagers sweated together to achieve a goal they had set themselves.

Emphasis Shifts to Increasing Incomes

The *Saemaul* Movement began with the improvement of the physical environment, but it developed into two other areas: the cultivation of moral standards and the raising of income. Gradually the emphasis was shifted from improving the environment to increasing incomes.

In the early 1970s, as a first step toward increasing incomes, the "unification rice strain" that guaranteed a larger crop was distributed to be grown communally. As a result, seeing ten to thirty farmers working together in a field became common. A young farmer conversant with agricultural skills was selected as the leader of a team that worked closely together, from seed selection to harvest. This cooperative method of farming contributed to the rapid spread of the new rice strain across the country. Between 1970 and 1977 the rice yield per hectare rose from 3.5 tons to 4.9 tons.

The next step was to incorporate the existing second Special Program to Increase Farmers' and Fishermen's Incomes into the *Saemaul* Movement. In addition, the government encouraged entrepreneurs to build factories in rural areas. This policy raised farmers' incomes dramatically.

Multifaceted Impact of the Movement: Living Standards and Income Distribution

In sum, rural incomes increased to the level of city laborers' incomes: farmers were no longer dependent on rice and barley as the proportion of their income from other products increased; and with the increase in the amount of income earned outside farming, the income gap between farmers who owned different amounts of land was narrowed.

Several factors contributed to the increase in farm incomes. First, a new strain of rice that had a higher yield was introduced in the early

1970s. Second, the government provided financial assistance to maintain a high government purchase price for rice. Third, individual farm's resources that were traditionally set aside for grain were now diverted to products that commanded higher prices. Fourth, with the spread of urbanization and industrialization to rural areas, income from sources other than farming increased. Finally, the government and farmers invested heavily in the *Saemaul* Movement. When their incomes increased, farmers began to save and worked harder to save more.

Radical Transformation of the Rural Life Style and Landscape

Several other remarkable changes occurred of the *Saemaul* Movement.

- Almost all villages became accessible by car. Previously, to get to a village from a national or regional highway almost always entailed going along a narrow, winding road, and often the local brook had no bridge over it. However, by the end of the 1970s almost all villages enjoyed bus service, taxi companies had sprouted up in small towns, and one could see mopeds everywhere.
- The embankments of all small rivers were repaired. Before the movement small rivers frequently flooded villages during the rainy season.
- The prevalent thatched roofs (80 percent of total houses) could no longer be seen in the villages. They had given way to tiles or roofing slates. Crumbling houses were rebuilt, and the village roads were widened and paved. In addition, sewers were installed and trees were planted to improve the environment.
- Every household was connected to running water. In the past, the rural population had used communal wells, which were easily contaminated, and women had to spend a great deal of time carrying water home. Under the movement some villages built reservoirs and the water was piped to individual homes. Others installed pipes in a deep well and pumped water to individual houses. With this modernization, the incidence of waterborne diseases such as typhoid fever and dysentery fell, and rural women spent less time and energy hauling water.
- Electricity reached every village. Until the end of the 1960s only 20 percent of farm households had electricity. In the early 1970s the *Saemaul* Movement gave priority to electrification in motivated vil-

lages. By 1979 98.7 percent of the rural households enjoyed electricity, the exceptions being a few isolated island villages.
- Telephones reached into the smallest villages. Until 1970 only one-tenth of rural villages had telephones, but by 1978 all administrative districts down to the smallest had telephones, and medium-size administrative districts had telephone exchange services. Island villages were provided with radio-telephone service by 1979 in the ratio of one instrument per fifty residents.
- Every village built a town meeting hall to provide the villagers with a place to work together in winter or to have meetings year round. The hall was equipped with a kitchen where women could cook together to save labor during busy farming seasons. Some halls were even equipped with a store, a nursery, and a playground.

The Status of Women

Among the effects of the *Saemaul* Movement, perhaps the most intangible, was the enhanced status of rural women. Traditionally, men made decisions about village matters; however, the *Saemaul* Movement changed that tradition because every household had to send a representative to movement meetings, and that forced the inclusion of women. As time went on, it was clear that things went more smoothly when women participated in discussions. Eventually each village selected both a male and a female leader.

Each village also organized a women's group, and these women became the pillar of the movement. The groups started the "save the rice and deposit" drive to raise funds. Each member set aside a spoonful of uncooked rice every time she cooked rice, and the women collected the rice every month and sold it to raise funds for the group's activities.

In the past, farmers rarely used financial institutions and almost no one possessed a savings book. With the save the rice and deposit drive each farm household had a savings account, and the amount of money deposited with the Agricultural Cooperative increased. Until the mid-1960s, 70 percent of agricultural loans were derived from government or banking funds, but by the middle of the 1970s only 20 percent came from these sources. Thus the rural women's groups save the rice and deposit drive also helped to improve agricultural banking as well as individual household prosperity.

These same groups of women also started a campaign to break their husbands' gambling and drinking habits, which monopolized their time during the winter. Their campaign successfully reduced the men's idleness during the off-season.

The most invaluable lesson for the rural population, however, was that they acquired the democratic process of discussion and agreement. In village meeting places, the *Saemaul* projects and women's group activities were recorded and filed together with basic statistics about the village.

The President's Creative Leadership

One of the president's economic aides once said, "President Park was born with the characteristics of a *Saemaul* leader and was the driving force for the *Saemaul* training," with which I agree wholeheartedly. The president himself composed the delightful *Saemaul* Song. When the song spread far and wide he composed another song, My Country, that inspired patriotism.

In June 1971 two farmers were selected to talk about their villages' successes at one of the Cabinet's monthly economic meetings chaired by the president. Afterwards success stories of the *Saemaul* movement in factories and schools were regularly presented at these meetings. The leaders were awarded with a *Saemaul* medal during the meeting, and later had lunch with their regional government officials to discuss future endeavors. From the mid-1970s, the Ministry of Home Affairs reported the progress of the *Saemaul* Movement at every monthly cabinet meeting held at the Blue House to solve any problems and to promote cooperation among the ministries. The president visited *Saemaul* villages whenever he could during his tours of the country, and he was delighted every time he heard that things were going well.

There were some projects the president had started during his eighteen-year regime that might deserve criticism, but I firmly believe that the *Saemaul* Movement was one of his masterpieces, designed for the well-being of the rural population, and eventually for all Koreans.

Reforestation Projects and Policies

While he was in office, one of the projects President Park pursued was the greening of the mountains. Although creating forests out of barren mountains usually takes tens of years, the president successfully turned the Korean countryside green within a generation.

Background

The trees on Korea's mountains had always been sparse compared to the dense forests of North Korea, and to make matters worse, from 1941 the Japanese cut down most of the trees to build ships. Then toward the end of the Japanese occupation, all kinds of forest products, including bark, leaves, sap, and roots, were shipped off for use in Japan. After the Korean War the forests became even more barren as people cut down more trees for fuel and construction materials. By the end of the 1950s, people had begun to realize that reforestation was now an urgent matter.

Forests not only produce useful products, but also prevent flooding, stabilize the soil, and beautify the scenery. Most Korean mountains are made of granite and granite gneiss that are easily erodible, and rivers tend to be short and fast flowing. As a result, during the rainy season in July and August floods, erosion, and landslides were common, alternating with periods of severe drought during the dry months. Until the mid-1970s floods and droughts occurred frequently, and the barren mountains were the main culprits.

Legislative Measures

In 1961, President Park's first year in office, the Forestry Law was enacted, followed by the Act on Forestry Product Control and the Hunting Law, which limited the period, place, and kind of hunting. In 1962 the Erosion Control Project Act was enacted, which allowed the government to carry out erosion control projects without property owners' consent, but such owners were paid compensation for any financial loss they might have incurred.

The traditional heating system, ondol, used all kinds of forest products, from tree roots to fallen leaves. Years of scraping the earth for fuel had left the mountain soils exposed and crumbling. Thus, an enormous amount of mountain terrain needed erosion control measures before reforestation attempts could be made. Because of the lack of funds, the government resorted to an emergency law that required compulsory service from February 1963 to December 1964, when large-scale erosion control activities were conducted throughout the country.

Traditionally, slash-and-burn farmers lived deep in the mountains, left the earth wasted, and caused many fires. In 1966 the Act on Dissolving Fire Farming was enacted to encourage these farmers to relocate. In 1967 the Forestry Administration, until then a bureau of the Ministry of Agriculture and Forestry, was elevated to the Office of Forestry as a separate institution with three bureaus and twelve divisions.

In summary, the basis for forestry administration was developed and forestry policy was established during the 1960s. Every year government officials, soldiers, and students observed Erosion Control Day on March 15 and Arbor Day on April 5 by planting seeds and trees. However, the mountains could not be brought back to life overnight because of the utter devastation of the mountain soils.

Distributing Fast-Growing Trees and Disseminating Know-How

In 1967 Dr. Hyun of Seoul National University succeeded in developing a fast-growing aspen, dubbed Hyun aspen, which was suitable for the Korean mountains. In 1969 the Office of Forestry distributed chestnut, walnut, and jujube trees along with instructions about new cultivation techniques. Hyun aspens, walnuts, jujubes, and insect-resistant chestnut trees began to transform the Korean mountainsides.

I had some basic knowledge about trees, but after I became the chief of staff to the president I began to read forestry textbooks and to visit the Forestry Experiment Station in Kwangnung on Sundays to talk with the staff about new techniques. By observing the progress made between 1970 and 1972, I judged that all Koreans should become involved in projects to "green the mountains." To make Erosion Control Day and Arbor Day meaningful, careful preparation and the dissemination of accurate basic knowledge were essential.

I believed that training local officials, teachers, and *Saemaul* leaders was the most effective way to educate the public. I also thought that transferring the Office of Forestry temporarily to the Ministry of Home Affairs would be wise because it could operate more effectively within the ministry's framework, given that it had administrative units concerned with all, even the smallest, communities. I visited Hyun at his laboratory at the Forestry Breeding Research Institute in Suwon and asked for his opinion. He agreed that placing the Office of Forestry under the Ministry of Home Affairs might be a good way to achieve rapid results. I suggested the move to the president, and he promptly gave approval to go ahead. Years later, in 1987, when the environmental goals had been achieved, the Office of Forestry was moved back to the Ministry of Agriculture and Forestry.

Implementation of My Proposal

To effect the transfer of the Office of Forestry, the National Assembly revised the Government Organization Law in 1972, with effect in January 1973. With the transfer of the Office of Forestry, the cities' and provinces' forestry or reforestation departments were promoted one level. Each administrative unit now had forestry officials, and various institutions, such as provincial forestry agencies, erosion control agencies, and provincial forestry experiment stations, were created under the leadership of the provincial administrator. The system to educate the public was in place, from the Office of Forestry in the central government to the smallest local administrative unit.

As the police were under the jurisdiction of the Ministry of Home Affairs, the police force was in charge of monitoring the forests. Local civil servants were responsible for regular forest administration, while forestry officials handled the dissemination of reforestation skills. With this comprehensive system, an effective reforestation program was launched. I established the Reforestation Hot Line at the Presidential Secretarial Office to follow progress and support the various levels of forestry administration nationwide.

Immediately on taking office, the new administrator of the Office of Forestry devised a ten-year plan (1973–82). The first step in the two-step plan was to promote erosion control projects in the mountains and to plant fast-growing trees. The second step involved planting slow-growing trees that would yield larger economic gains in the future.

The goals of the first ten-year plan were realized in 1978, four years ahead of schedule, and a number of major changes took place during the plan's implementation. To begin with, Arbor Day had been merely a ceremonial occasion, and tree planting took only half a day. From 1973, each region chose a People's Planting Day between March 21 and April 20 based on its climate, and devoted an entire day to planting trees. Before, trees had been planted following a short explanation at the sites, but now all government forestry officials were mobilized to educate the public on how to handle and plant saplings. During the first stage, the ratio of quick-growing and fruit trees planted to slow-growing trees was seven to three. In the past, forty-two kinds of trees had been planted at random, but now only ten varieties were selected for planting: chestnuts, Italian poplars, aspens, paulownias, alders, and acacias were the fast-growing trees planted, and pines, larches, Japanese cedars, and Japanese cypresses were the slow-growing trees used. These saplings were distributed along with specific planting instructions.

Incorporation into the Saemaul Movement

Tree planting was incorporated into the *Saemaul* Movement, with the focus on promoting tree nurseries and collective planting activities in villages. The village nurseries were a source of good saplings and generated additional income for farmers. The government supplied superior seeds and equipment, taught skills, and purchased the saplings at high prices. For collective planting, appropriate trees were selected for each region, and *Saemaul* leaders supervised planting in spring and the examination of trees in the autumn. The Office of Forestry appointed three graduates of agricultural high schools to each administrative unit to cultivate a demonstration forest in a village and to educate the public. In addition, *Saemaul* leaders were trained to maintain tree nurseries and were taught planting techniques at the Provincial Forestry Experiment Stations.

Property owners in the mountains were ordered to reforest, and if they did not comply, the government had the right to plant trees on their property. When the owner did not live in the area, villagers were allowed to plant trees, and when they were later cut, the profits were to be shared by the owner and the villagers. To achieve erosion control and reforestation simultaneously, the government paid wages to those working on erosion control projects.

Traditionally, Korean farmers and urban households depended on the forest for fuel. In 1957 the nineteen-hole coal briquette was introduced and bringing wood to the cities for fuel was prohibited. Farmers not only cut trees, but also gathered fallen leaves for fuel, which contributed to soil erosion. Without a reasonable policy to supply fuel to rural areas, reforestation and the establishment of forestry resources were impossible. For that reason, the government started creating forests intended specifically for fuel in 1959.

Promotion of the Forests-for-Fuel Concept

President Park promoted the concept of forests-for-fuel as part of both the First and Second Five-Year Economic Development plans, which started in 1962 and 1967, respectively. However, according to a 1972 survey, half of the areas designated as forest-for-fuel proved to be failures. Many reasons might have accounted for the lack of success, but the main cause was the property owners' reluctance to plant trees that could be used for fuel, such as acacia, alder, and pine. They preferred to use their mountain property for activities that yielded larger profits.

In 1974, President Park ordered the development of forests-for-fuel in various sites near villages and along roads, and rivers. Until that time such forests had only been allowed in the mountains. Research efforts were also under way to develop a more effective furnace. In 1973 researchers developed a new furnace that reduced fuel consumption by 30 percent, and between 1974 and 1976 the government promoted the replacement of furnaces of all 6.7 million farm households. From 1975 additional sources of fuel were readily available from trees in the village cooperative nurseries.

The creation of forests-for-fuel was completed by the end of 1977, ahead of schedule. With the increased supply of wood from nursery projects and the spread of electricity, coal, and oil to the countryside, the problem of a lack of fuel in the countryside was completely solved by 1977.

The Office of Forestry launched large-scale care projects and protection policies, including supplementary planting, fertilization, weeding, pruning, and tending of fuel and other special-purpose trees. The supplementary planting was done only in areas where the survival rate of planted trees was less than 80 percent. The areas near the young trees were weeded twice a year as a communal village project and the weeds were used for compost. By performing these tasks government officials, *Saemaul* leaders, and villagers accumulated skills. Forest products were gathered twice a year and shared among the gatherers. In this way, trees were tended, forests were protected, and fuel was secured.

Every year officials from local and central authorities checked the planted trees. Villagers attended evaluation sessions at the examination sites, which helped raise their consciousness about planting and taking care of trees afterwards as well as improving their skills.

The Forestry Breeding Institute studied the use of fertilizer and found out that fertilizing planted trees for a certain period of time was effective. For example, the Hyun aspen grew 66 percent faster when 200 grams of chemical fertilizer were applied three years running after the planting. In July 1976 the president directed that forest trees be fertilized to increase productivity. Fertilizer specifically formulated for forestry trees was used, and the public realized that trees in the forests needed fertilizer just like other crops.

As for gathering fallen leaves, the president ordered the eradication of this practice in early 1975 during his visit to the Ministry of Home Affairs, because the supply of fuel was now sufficient. The local police were responsible for investigating violations. Soon the pile of fallen leaves on the ground had the same effect as fertilizer, thereby contributing to the faster greening of the mountains.

In 1977, the government chose the first Saturday of November as Forest Tending Day to encourage the long-term care of trees after planting, and on that day the public participated in such activities as examining and fertilizing trees, taking preventive action against insects and diseases, and pruning branches.

The Emphasis Shifts to Raising Farm Incomes

In drafting the ten-year Reforestation Plan (1973–82), the ratio between fast-growing trees and trees to provide long-term benefits was an important feature of the plan. As mentioned earlier, the initial ratio was seven to three, but it was to be reversed at the end of the first plan. When those involved realized that the plan's goals could be reached ahead of schedule, President Park repeatedly emphasized that the direction of forestry policy should shift so as to emphasize the planting of trees that would raise farmers' incomes. Accordingly, the Office of Forestry established eighty-six Economic Forest Complexes, and by 1979, the total size of such complexes had reached 2,000 hectares.

To maintain soil quality and prevent disease while changing the kind and ratio of trees grown in the mountains, the government banned large-scale tree felling and encouraged logging in alternate rows. The hills between Kyongju and Yangsan on the Seoul-Pusan expressway became a showcase for different the varieties of logging trees. Also instead of large-scale coniferous forests, a combination of evergreen and deciduous forests was encouraged.

Once the newly planted chestnut trees were producing an ample harvest, President Park directed the Korean Institute of Science and Technology to invent a chestnut peeler and the Economic Staff Office to the President to develop chestnut products. The institute came up with a simple peeler and the Economic Staff Office developed high quality marrons glacés for export. The president said that when he was small he used to come home from school and vainly search the kitchen for something to snack on, and he was happy that farm children could now snack on roasted or steamed chestnuts year round.

A Success Story

According to 1984 forestry statistics, 51 percent of trees were less than ten years old, and 84 percent of the entire stock was less than 20 years old. In other words, 84 percent of Korea's forestry resources had been planted during President Park's regime. When President Park was assassinated in 1979, Takeo Fukuda, a former Japanese prime minister, paid condolences to me (I was ambassador to Japan at the time), saying that the success of reforestation in Korea during the Park regime had been more difficult to achieve and was more valuable than any other of the regime's economic achievements.

Construction of a Network of Expressways

With the successful progress of the First Five-Year Economic Development Plan (1962–66), the volume of traffic soared. Around 1964 the national economy showed an unexpected surge, but the capacity of the transportation sector was so inadequate that transportation problems became a major roadblock to steady economic growth. Furthermore, repeated price hikes resulted. During the meetings of economic ministers, the theme of how to allocate major materials such as grain, coal, fertilizer, and cement to limited train wagons was one of the most important topics, and caused heated arguments among the ministers. Obviously structural reform in the transportation sector was urgent.

World Bank Report on Transportation Problems

The government had the Ministry of Transportation ask a foreign institute to study transportation problems in Korea. The Ministry of Transportation chose the International Bank for Reconstruction and Development (IBRD), partly because it was an international authority, and partly because Koreans hoped to obtain IBRD loans for future transportation investments. The contract for the study was signed in September 1965, and the IBRD survey team reviewed the transportation system from November 1965 to June 1966.

The report noted that despite efforts during the previous twelve years, Korea's road network was in poor shape. While the quality of construction was generally good, the roads had not been modernized (blacktopped). The most salient feature of surface transportation in Korea was the imbalance between railways and roads. In 1965 the total length of railway track was 3,000 kilometers, while the total number of automobiles amounted to 41,000, or 1 car for every 700 persons; one of the lowest ratios in the world.

What the survey team recommended most strongly was that the transportation system, which until then had relied heavily on the railways, should be transformed into one centered on the highways, given that the volume of freight was expected to grow at 10.2 percent per year and the number of passengers at 11.5 percent per year. The IBRD team members warned that an inadequate transportation system would create serious hurdles to economic development. They recommended paving 3,300 kilometers of highway between major cities during the Second Five-Year Economic Development Plan. They also suggested that the different transportation agencies should be reorganized into a single body, and that the Road Division in the National Land Preservation Bureau of the Ministry of Construction should be promoted to the bureau level. Their recommendations provided a fresh look at the situation because they pointed out matters that the government had not even been aware of. The government adopted most of their recommendations.

The Ministry of Construction developed a plan to build 143 kilometers of toll roads in ten areas. Eight of these projects would consist of paving existing highways, and the Seoul-Suwon and Seoul-Inchon highways were to be built. The IBRD team expressed doubts about this plan, saying that toll roads were premature for Korea because most drivers would choose unpaved roads to avoid paying tolls. However, they thought building the two new highways was a good idea, and that these roads would eventually become large-scale expressways. It was the first time they had used the term expressway.

World Bank Skeptical of the Feasibility of Expressways

The IBRD survey team did not recommend, or even hint, that Korea's transportation and traffic difficulties should be solved by a network of expressways, although their evaluation covered up to the period of the Third Five-Year Economic Development Plan (1972–76). It is true that the IBRD team gave us the opportunity to become aware of the problems and helped us greatly in establishing road policies. However, they did not recommend constructing a network of expressways, perhaps because they believed that such factors as the limited national supply of power, the shortage of equipment, and the lack of technology implied an inability for Korea to embark on this kind of undertaking. They probably assumed that Korea would develop at a rate similar to that of other developing countries, and could not have imagined that Korea would achieve rapid economic development and manage to build expressways in a short period of time at a fraction of the cost in industrial countries.

The President Decides to Build a Network of Expressways

When President Park had the IBRD report in his hand, he was confident that the Second Five-Year Economic Development Plan would exceed its goals just as the First Five-Year Economic Development Plan had. He believed that the demand for transportation would be far greater than the IBRD team members had estimated, because they had based their calculations on the goals of the First and Second Five-Year Development Plans.

The completion of the Wulsan oil refinery in 1964 enabled the mass production of asphalt. Cement production facilities were also expanded and construction skills improved thanks to Korean companies' road construction assignments overseas. In 1967 President Park decided to push the construction of the expressways despite the numerous difficulties this would entail.

President Park made his expressway plan public in April 1967 as part of his election campaign. At a press conference a month later he explained his comprehensive plan for building expressways and ports and developing rivers. He said that the expressways should radiate from Seoul to Inchon, Kangnung, Pusan, and Mokpo. He noted that constructing an expressway is a mammoth project that requires a vast amount of human resources, equipment, funds, and materials, but that Korea was ready for such an undertaking.

On May 1, 1967, the ground-breaking ceremony for the Seoul-Inchon expressway was held. In November 1967 the minister of construction reported a long-term road development plan for the Second and Third Five-Year Economic Development plans during a meeting at the Blue House. The plan included construction of Seoul-Inchon, Seoul-Pusan, Seoul-Kangnung, Taejon-Mokpo, and east and south coast expressways. The plan also included details of how the funds would be raised.

The president directed that the Seoul-Pusan expressway be constructed, with the aim of speeding up economic development by connecting the country's two major economic centers. The mood inside and outside the country was predominantly pessimistic about the undertaking, but the president continued in his resolve, saying that domestic funds, skills, and efforts would be invested in the construction because the expressway would symbolize Korea's modernization. He emphasized that developing roads was the most effective way to solve transportation problems with limited funds, and was a more effective investment than constructing ports or railways. He went on to say that with the expressway various industries would develop, regional development would accelerate, and people's options would increase.

The Seoul-Inchon expressway was undertaken because of large increases in transportation needs following the success of the First Five-Year Economic Development Plan. The hope was that connecting Seoul to Inchon, the second largest port and the gateway to Seoul, would enhance the success of the Second Five-Year Economic Development Plan.

Choice of the Seoul-Pusan Expressway as the First Project

The Seoul-Pusan expressway was chosen as the first project for the following reasons:

- Of the total population, 63 percent lived in areas through which the expressway was to pass, and by connecting the two major cities, where 66 percent of the GNP and 81 percent of industrial production were concentrated, more economic benefits were expected.
- Eighty-one percent of Korea's automobiles were in the area the proposed expressway was to pass through. Furthermore, the rate of increase in the number of cars in those areas was much higher than in other areas.

- The new expressway could be built parallel to the railway, but the authorities believed that this would be more beneficial than damaging, and would relieve reliance on railway transport.
- The efficiency of exports and imports would be increased by connecting the two major ports of Pusan and Inchon via Seoul.

Estimates of Construction Costs

For the reasons cited the president involved himself in the project. The most pressing problem was fundraising. According to the case studies the president had collected, the cost of expressways in the industrial countries was astronomical. According to the IBRD report, the cost of the six-lane expressway that was being constructed between Tokyo and Nagoya was W800 million per kilometer, or W500 million if it were reduced to four lanes. If these figures were applied to the Seoul-Pusan expressway, the 428 kilometers would have required W214 billion, 30 percent more than Korea's total national budget for 1967.

After directing the Ministry of Construction to build the Seoul-Pusan expressway, the president decided to gather estimates from relevant government offices and the army. He also asked for a cost estimate from the Hyundai construction company because it had built an IBRD-financed expressway in Thailand. The president decided to reduce costs in a number of ways: by using asphalt pavement instead of the cement most industrial countries use, by going without electric lights and telephones along the expressway, and by omitting a center divider except in especially dangerous spots.

Government offices, the army, and Hyundai submitted estimates based on a four-lane road. The estimated costs varied as follows:

Ministry of Construction	W65 billion
Army Engineering Office	W49 billion
Ministry of Finance	W33 billion
Hyundai Construction Co.	W28 million
Metropolitan City of Seoul	W18 billion
Economic Planning Board	No estimate submitted

To devise the construction plans, the president had three army engineering officers and a ministry of construction employee on duty at the

Blue House. He personally directed them to review the possible routes, calculate construction costs, and examine the purchase of the land this would entail. His own estimate of the construction costs was W30 billion based on the highest and lowest of the estimates and that of Hyundai.

Project Planning and Financing

The Ministry of Construction could not undertake construction singlehandedly because the Road Bureau had not yet been set up in the ministry. The ministry's National Land Preservation Bureau was responsible not only for roads, but also for urban housing and ports. Thus the president founded the National Key Expressway Construction Planning Board on December 15, 1967, which consisted of relevant government officials and construction company representatives. He directed the board to set up a plan based on 33 billion (W30 billion plus 10 percent). In other words, the cost estimate was not based on the project's scope but on the amount of funds available.

In February 1968 the funding plan for the Seoul-Pusan expressway was finalized at the economic ministers' meeting. The revenues would be derived as follows: W13.9 billion from a tax on petroleum products, W6.0 billion from transit duties, W 8.4 billion from the sale of imported grain on a credit basis, W2.7 billion from the claims funds from Japan, W1.5 billion from tolls, and W600 million from the existing budget.

The President's Secret Plan to Purchase Land

The president secretly worked on the purchase of the necessary land. As a former artillery officer he knew how to read maps. He studied the map of Korea and drew in several possible routes. After working on the routes between Seoul and Suwon, the first leg of the route, he secretly summoned two commercial bank presidents and asked them to appraise the prices of land along the possible route.

On receiving their reports, he summoned the minister of construction, the mayor of Seoul, and the governor of Kyonggi-do province to the Blue House. He explained how the route was to be decided and directed the mayor of Seoul and the governor of Kyonggi-do Province to speed up the purchase of the land. He showed them the appraisal reports and explained that the average price of land between Seoul and Suwon was around W170 to W180 per pyong (3.3 square meters). However, land prices near Seoul could be higher, and W300 per pyong would be allotted. After securing the land, the governor could use any funds left over on those projects he deemed necessary, for example, reorganizing farmland, improving water facilities, or repairing roads. He directed that the work be done within a week, explaining to the shocked mayor and governor that otherwise land prices would skyrocket. He added that they should at least secure permission to start construction from the landowners within a week and that the final details could be worked out later, after breaking ground for the expressway.

Toward the end of 1967 the president called a meeting of provincial governors' and directed them to purchase land for the expressway. They were to purchase the land at market prices as soon as possible following the example of the governor of Kyonggi-do province, and if they had funds left over after the purchase they too were free to use them for regional development projects.

Implementation

By the end of 1967 the necessary land for the section of the expressway from Seoul to Suwon was secured, and in January 1968 the Seoul-Taejon route was finalized. On January 29, 1968, the National Key Expressway Construction Planning Board was disbanded, and the Seoul-Pusan Expressway Construction Project Office was established in the Ministry of Construction. On February 1, 1968, a ceremony to mark the start of construction was held at the spot where the toll booths would eventually be located. Dignitaries, construction people, and citizens attended the ceremony.

The next hurdle after securing the necessary funds was the importation of construction equipment. The Seoul-Inchon expressway, already under construction, was moving slowly because of the lack of heavy equipment. According to the IBRD report, in 1965 Korea had only 1,647 pieces of heavy equipment, most of which were outdated.

As an emergency measure, the government made agreements with major foreign companies in France, Sweden, the United Kingdom, and the United States to purchase equipment at average export prices in the second half of 1967. To pay for the equipment Korean construction companies sought foreign commercial loans.

Another pressing task was to secure supervisors and quality control personnel. Korea had few road construction experts, and of these few almost none had any experience in expressway construction. The matter was more complicated because various legs of the 428-kilometer route were to be constructed simultaneously, with completion in three years.

The president decided to take advantage of army engineering officers and to train college graduates who majored in civil engineering as supervisors. To begin with twenty-two officers, all graduates of the Military Academy, were selected for special training, followed by twelve Reserve Officer Training Corps officers. Later civil engineering graduates were selected and trained on a continuous basis.

Before the construction of the Seoul-Pusan expressway, civil engineering projects in Korea had not used quality control testing personnel. To obtain such personnel, fifty college and technical high school graduates who had majored in engineering were selected and trained, followed by other recruits later.

The young supervisors and testing personnel did their job conscientiously, raising the quality of the construction. Some of them would later work on foreign construction sites, building a reputation for Korea's construction skills.

In July 1970 the completion ceremony took place, during which I witnessed young supervisors shedding tears while the president awarded medals to them. I felt that their tears were not only because of the honor of being given medals, but also because of the realization that they had fulfilled their responsibility despite all kinds of difficulties.

Another point to note is that army engineering soldiers were mobilized for constructing those sections of road that required specialized civil engineering skills. Given their superior efficiency, construction costs were lowered considerably.

Completion

The first leg of the road, from Seoul to Osan, was opened in December 1968, only eleven months after the ground-breaking ceremony. The president ordered that the construction period be shortened by one year, to finish on June 30, 1970. The Taejon-Taegu leg, the most difficult section because it required more long bridges and tunnels than any other section, was the last to be completed. It was finished on July 7, 1970, two years and five months from the day of the start of construction.

The final cost of the expressway amounted to W42.9 billion, more than the estimate because of inflation during the construction period and several design changes. However, the cost of W100 million per kilometer was only one-fifth the cost of Japan's Tokyo-Nagoya expressway using the cost for four lanes (the Tokyo-Nagoya expressway actually has six lanes). The Seoul-Pusan expressway holds a world record in that it was built at the lowest cost, in the shortest time, and using only domestically available skills.

After the completion of the Seoul-Pusan expressway eight more expressways were completed between May 1, 1967, and December 14, 1977.

Impact on Socioeconomic Development

The two epochal events in Korean transportation history are construction of the railway in 1900 and of the expressways around 1970. To be more precise, history was made on December 21, 1968, when the Seoul-Inchon and Seoul-Sewon expressways were opened. At a time when the main roads were still unpaved, the expressways were a dream come true. They transformed Korea's entire socioeconomic structure and were one of the vital factors in what is called the Korean Miracle, a sustained high rate of growth over almost four decades. Their impact on socioeconomic development was multidimensional.

The expressways exerted influence on various aspects of Korean life: politics, the economy, society, and culture. In terms of economic effects, the expressways not only improved transportation and traffic flow, but also improved the distribution structure and helped develop agriculture and industry. Other effects included changing people's awareness of social and cultural matters and promoting tourism. Let me explain these effects in detail.

After the expressways opened, a change of revolutionary magnitude took place in the structure and system of transportation. By 1975 the roles of the railway and the expressways were reversed, and the expressways took more than two-thirds of the total freight traffic. More than 56 percent of the vehicles on the expressways were trucks. Clearly if the first expressway had not been started of 1967, the economic development of the 1970s would have been dramatically slowed down because of transportation difficulties.

The expressways also helped raise farmers' and fishermen's incomes. The "silver revolution," growing vegetables and fruit in greenhouses, took place after polyethylene film became easily available following construction of the petrochemical factories, almost at the same time as the first expressway was completed. As a result, vegetables, fruit, and flowers grown around the country reached major cities in one day year round, increasing farm incomes. Dairy farming also raised farmers' incomes thanks to processing facilities located near the expressways. Fishermen's incomes increased because now fresh fish could reach Seoul overnight, which meant the fish fetched better prices, and were no longer prevented from reaching the cities by bad winter weather that often blocked local highways.

Another benefit of the initial expressway was the congregation of factories within a thirty-kilometer strip on either side of the route. This lowered production costs by reducing transportation time and costs. Also factories could take advantage of the low wages in the countryside. The inland cities that had been slow to industrialize were transformed because the expressways helped spread out industrial parks. In this way, the concentration of population was diffused naturally. For example, Yochon Petrochemical Industrial Complex and Kwangyang Integrated Steel Mill in the southwest coast were made possible by the new expressway passing their sites.

The expressways also serve a strategic purpose. In case of emergency, military divisions can be quickly moved to where they are needed; supplementary personnel, equipment, and munitions can be delivered; refugees can be evacuated; and aircraft can take off and land on the expressways. During the Korean War, United Nations troops were hindered by the bad roads.

Finally, one could read any part of the country in a day, bringing the regions closer together and spurring economic development. In other words, the expressways helped to promote psychological and cultural homogeneity.

The Principle of Opening First and Repairing Later

When the president revealed his idea of building expressways in 1967 he encountered much opposition. Some people insisted that the funds for the expressways should be used for the repair and paving of the existing roads, while others asserted that the funds would be used more effectively if they were allocated to other purposes. Some people even claimed that the new expressways would merely become tourist movers, benefiting only car owners and tour buses. When the public began to experience the benefits of the expressways, however, more people supported them. After the president's assassination in 1979, criticism surfaced because of the high cost of repairing the Seoul-Pusan expressway, where truck traffic is heavy.

The Seoul-Pusan expressway cost about one-fifth of what an industrial country would have spent, which would have been around W214 billion. This sum was W50 billion more than Korea's entire national budged for 1967, ands W70 billion more than the cost of building all the expressways in Korea.

The president promoted the principle of opening first, and repairing later. He believed that the expressways could be improved as the toll revenues accumulated, saying that good repair would raise the quality of the roads to the level of that in the industrial countries.

At first, the IBRD was very negative about granting loans to Korea for expressway construction because of its traditional negative view of building expressways in developing countries. Thus the Seoul-Pusan, Taejon-Chonju, and Singal-Saemal expressways had to be built using only domestic funds. However, the IBRD changed its views when the Seoul-Pusan expressway was successfully completed and proved effective. The IBRD responded by granting loans for the remaining expressways.

In February 1969 the government established the Korean Road Corporation to oversee the construction, maintenance, and repair of toll expressways. The corporation is responsible for managing and maintaining all the expressways launching some new expressways. Except for 1969, the year of its inception, the corporation has generated a considerable profit every year, even after making the necessary repairs.

How President Park Came Up with the Expressway Project

After I became chief of staff to the president in 1969, I often heard the behind-the-scenes story about the president's involvement in getting the expressways built. Park saw an expressway for the first time during the Korean War when he was sent to an artillery school in the United States for training. In December 1964 he visited the Federal Republic of Germany as Korea's head of state and was deeply impressed with Germany's expressways. According to the interpreter who accompanied him, the German president mentioned that President Park was to travel on the autobahn from Bonn to Köln and informed him that the Germans were very proud of having built the first expressway in the world because it was a symbol of German revival.

During Park's 160 kilometer per hour trip on the 20-kilometer expressway, he stopped the car twice so that he could study the center divider, the road surface, and the crossing facilities. He asked his German guide, the chief of protocol to the German president, many questions. Luckily, the guide was an economist, conversant with various aspects of expressways, ranging from construction to funding. He unfolded a map of Germany, and pointed to the expressways criss-crossing the country. The federal chancellor of Germany was Erhart, the man who had achieved the "miracle of the Rhine" as an economic minister. When President Park had a meeting with Erhart he asked numerous questions about the revival of the German economy and received detailed replies. Erhart said that the only way to beat the communists as a divided nation was to build a strong economy, and explained how the autobahns had contributed to the German economy. President Park later said that he vividly remembered Erhart saying that whenever he drove on or off an expressway, he paid a mental tribute to that excellent system of roads.

10

President Park's Vision and Leadership

President Park read voraciously about Korean history and held a specific historical viewpoint. According to him, the Korean people possess a history, tradition, and culture that are by no means inferior to those of other peoples'. He believed that the recurrence of various invasions and periods of disgrace during the Choson Dynasty (1392–1910) could have been prevented if the people of Korea had tried hard to avoid repeating the same mistakes. For example, the court did not agree with the proposal to mobilize 100,000 soldiers ten years before the Imjin Japanese invasion (1592), resulting in an eight-year war that devastated the country. Twenty years later, the Pyongja Chinese invasion occurred because the court and the people did not emphasize the prevention of further foreign invasions. Afterwards Korea had to pay tribute to China. Taewongun ruled Korea in the latter part of the nineteenth century. He tried to eliminate corrupt practices, but employed a strict closed-door policy, whereas Japan opened its doors and accepted Western culture with open arms. Instead of modernizing the country, Taewongun was busily engaged in a squabble for power with his daughter-in-law.

After liberalization in 1945 Koreans fought among themselves and split into leftists and rightists, which resulted in the country's division, whereas the Austrians kept their country intact after having been partitioned and occupied by France, the Soviet Union, the United Kingdom, and the United States. Then the Korean War broke out, leaving the Korean peninsula utterly devastated.

The Reunification Policy and Its Rationale

President Park formulated a reunification policy in the belief that reunification was the most urgent agenda for modern Koreans. He believed that the path toward reunification had three stages: economic development, accumulation of national power, and finally actual reunification. This was how he arrived at his focus on the economy. At the same time, faced with ceaseless invasion attempts by the People's Democratic Republic of Korea, he promoted a strong defense. He emphasized eliminating poverty and implemented various policies that would enable people to eat well. In this vein, one can understand his push for the export first policy, with the promotion of light and heavy and chemical industries.

In terms of security, he organized and armed a reserve army of 2.5 million soldiers, and promoted the defense industry and the modernization of the armed forces in response to ceaseless aggression by the North and Carter's plan to withdraw U.S. ground forces from the Korean peninsula.

Quick Decisionmaking and Prompt Implementation

President Park was a man of few words, who listened to others' opinions, and when a decision was arrived at after a discussion, he saw to it that it was carried out to completion. For example, for the simple project of developing underground water sources, he held dozens of meetings until all aspects of the project had been determined, and during implementation he often visited the project sites. When organizing the reserve army he met severe opposition from people who viewed his promotion of a reserve army as a political ploy to gain power. When they saw the results, however, many recognized the merits of this measure. It was the same with other projects: the First Five-Year Economic Development Plan, the normalization of relations with Japan, and the construction of Pohang Iron and Steel Mill and the expressways.

Innovative Ideas

President Park was a man of deep thoughts and creativity. Even after he went home to the inner quarters of the Blue House, he often made notes on matters he was considering and instructed his staff about them the next morning. His innovative ideas led to the reforestation of mountains, the planting of useful varieties of trees, the improvement of rural villages, the landscaping and placing of rest stops along the expressways, and the improvement of tourist complexes.

Personal Qualities

President Park was always neat and liked everything to be well organized. He took his own notes and organized and kept his own files. In the mid-1970s, he encouraged civil servants to wear shirts without neckties during the hot summer months. He himself designed several shirts and had his staff wear them first to see whether they looked neat. Whenever he had time to spare, he riffled through his files to reminisce about past difficulties. He had an incredible memory and was adept with numbers, often surprising ministers and experts.

Park was also a frugal man. Every day he ate rice mixed with barley to save on rice, his lunch was noodles, and his drink was the ordinary person's rice wine. He always used Korean-made products except for neckties, fountain pens, and electric shavers. The knot of a Korean-made necktie did not sit well, and the president instructed the Ministry of Commerce and Industry to support quality tie manufacture, but at that time Korea could not afford to pay the royalty for the lead-treatment technology needed for the knot. As for the fountain pen, the Pilot Company was fully supported, but they could not yet manufacture first-rate pens. He was very happy when OB Beer started producing white and red wine. He invited a foreign priest and a nun from a wine producing country for a drink at the Blue House, and had them taste both first-rate foreign wine and Korean wine. They said that the Korean white wine was good, and from then on the president served Korean wine whenever he entertained foreign dignitaries. For a Korean meal he used Popju, a traditional rice wine produced in Kyongju.

The china used in the Blue House was also made in Korea. When he first took office Park used regular china, but his wife encouraged a firm to produce bone china. Afterwards, Korean bone china was used in the Blue House and in overseas ambassadors' residences.

President Park had no trace of greed, something that became well known to the Korean people after his assassination. I accompanied the president in his numerous visits all over the country in his helicopter. When he looked down at high-rise buildings, beautiful rural houses, large and small factories, multipurpose dams, and river embankments he was always delighted as if they were all his personal belongings. He was never interested in his own property, giving his whole attention to the national economy.

People often made the criticism that President Park succeeded in economic development while neglecting the spiritual aspects of Korean life. It is true that he focused on economic growth in the belief that it was a shortcut to a peaceful reunification of the two Koreas. However, he also promoted the mental and spiritual elements of society because they were helpful in fighting communism and achieving a balance with the material aspects of modernization. Therefore, he composed the People's Education Charter, established the Academy of Korea Studies (liberally meaning the Korea Spiritual Culture Research Institute), and founded the *Saemaul* Movement to awaken people's spirit of self-help, independence, and cooperation.

The president was interested in historical examples of efforts to repel foreign invasions. He had various historical landmarks repaired or rebuilt to inspire patriotism.

He was also incredibly strong minded. The pressure on him as the final decisionmaker was hard to imagine. He worked day and night, sometimes holding meetings for ten to twenty days in a row and thinking about an issue constantly. At times he suffered from a duodenal ulcer, and recovery took several months.

Commitment to Social Justice and Austerity

The president had a special interest in farmers, factory workers, and those receiving an allowance to protect their livelihoods, and gave instructions about them quite often. He believed that when the number of farmers who owned land increased, communism would be defeated without difficulty, and that when the factory workers became the middle class, society would become more stable.

In 1974 rural incomes exceeded urban incomes after the implementation of various agricultural policies, and when he heard the news Park was happy beyond words. He was delighted that rural households could enjoy electricity because he remembered his own childhood, when he had to do without electric lights. When he heard that rural people could eat warm rice any time thanks to electric rice cookers and that they also enjoyed the comfort and convenience provided by electric fans and refrigerators, he expressed his happiness as if the farmers were members of his own family.

After black and white television sets had been widely distributed in the countryside, the electronics industry wanted to sell color television sets in the domestic market as a way to increase its exports through economies of scale. I suggested the idea several times to the president, but he maintained his stand that the rural population would be burdened by the pressure to buy new color television sets, and that the vivid and luxurious colors of city life brought to rural houses could adversely affect them by tempting rural youth to leave home for the cities.

He often had dinner with his aides, and sometimes the atmosphere became tense after a serious discussion of national affairs, but whenever he heard a concrete report of how the rural population was enjoying the fruits of development, he broke into a smile.

Whenever Park went on a tour of the various regions, he made it a rule to visit factories, engineering high schools, and job training centers. When he met the workers in a factory he encouraged them and visited their cafeterias, bath houses, and dormitories. He always inquired about their wages and welfare facilities. He supported the training of skilled workers because this would justify their asking for higher wages, helping them rise to the middle class.

He frowned at a luxurious owner's office in a factory, and he was pleased when he saw owners wearing the same uniform and eating in the same cafeteria as the workers. The president believed that when the owner led a frugal life and took good care of his workers, labor-management conflicts would be avoided even if the wages were low because of difficulties in the factory. He conceded that establishing a minimum wage was still a premature concept for Korea, but he instructed the Ministry of Health and Social Welfare and the Office of Labor to insist that the firms paying the lowest wages should be pressured to raise them to the average level of other firms in the same industry. He hoped that the *Saemaul* Movement in the factories could become the foundation of a Korean style of labor-management cooperation, promote productivity, and enhance workers' welfare.

As for those receiving livelihood protection allowances, he believed that they should be supported as well as the national budget permitted, with a focus on medical and economic assistance. As for the low-income groups, he stressed that they should be given work instead of free assistance from the government so as not to deprive them of the will to support themselves. Whenever possible he allocated *Saemaul* donations to labor projects for the low-income population.

I believe that President Park was endowed with the merits of a revolutionary, a soldier, an educator, and an administrator who laid a foundation for the revival of the Korean people and the modernization of the country.

Development Strategy and Policies and Their Implementation

Korea, with meager capital and technology, achieved economic success beginning in the 1960s through the implementation of unique policies. In 1962, the first year of the First Five-Year Economic Development Plan, Korean exports totaled US$55 million, its foreign currency holdings were US$168 million, and its growth rate was a mere 2.2 percent . In June 1963 foreign currency holdings dropped to US$114 million, and in November 1964, after a hard struggle, exports reached US$100 million. During this period, American economic aid still supported the economy, and foreign loans were absolutely necessary for economic development. Diplomatic ties with Japan were not normalized until 1965, and obtaining loans from European countries was impossible. The United State was the only country that Korea could depend on for loans, but as a poor country receiving American economic aid, Korea had low credibility in the international market.

Challenged by these conditions, the government created a system in which the Korean government or government-owned banks guaranteed loans, a measure unheard of in other countries. When private companies signed a loan contract in the form of a supplier's credit with a foreign financial institution that was approved by the Economic Planning Board and the National Assembly, the Korea Development Bank and the Bank of Korea guaranteed the loan. Later other banks were given the right to guarantee the loans and the Korea Exchange Bank took over the responsibility from the Bank of Korea. In this way, foreign lenders could grant loans without having to worry too much about individual companies' financial status.

Another aspect of note in the First Five-Year Economic Development Plan was that the country's leader paid close attention to every detail and encouraged the administrative and financial institutions to solve problems quickly. He established a plan situation room next to his office and frequently checked the progress of each project. He called relevant ministers when he found that a project was progressing slowly and brought up the matter during the monthly economic trend briefing and the government projects deliberation analysis meetings. He encouraged the ministries to support private projects in the belief that the successful completion contributed to national economic development.

The Ministry of Finance pressured the financial institutions to grant loans despite criticism of being heavy-handed, and the Ministry of Commerce and Industry ensured that projects listed in the plan were allocated construction materials. Because most Korean entrepreneurs had few financial assets, it was hard for the banks to guarantee foreign loans based on collateral. When a supported project ended in failure, some bank employees were held responsible for the shortage of collateral although all they had done was to follow government policy.

Once a planned project was completed, various ministries had to support it to guarantee its smooth operation. The failure of a project that had relied on a foreign loan could become a burden shouldered by the entire population, and Korean credibility could suffer in the international market, which would affect future loans. During the First Five-Year Economic Development Plan many factories faced slow sales or a temporary stop in their operations. For example, foreign companies, especially Japanese companies, would dump enough products to last six months to a year prior to the marketing of the same product by a Korean manufacturer who had just completed the construction of a factory. The tariff system that prevented dumping practices was yet to be established. The difficulty in sales posed a serious threat to it. The government supported the new factory with additional loans until the imports were consumed. After such an early blow, enterprises had to struggle for a number of years.

During the First and the Second Economic Development plans, criticism of monopolies and oligopolies often surfaced. Many enterprises owned the only factory in a certain industry. While the government was supposed to encourage new enterprises to participate in the same industry to discourage monopoly and oligopoly, the domestic market was too small to support such enterprises, and the firms were too small to compete with their counterparts on the international market. Consequently the authorities judged that excessive competition in the domestic market was unwise in light of limited domestic capital and foreign exchange holdings. The government supported the principle that prices and profits were to be controlled to prevent the evils of monopoly and oligopoly until enterprises grew to international levels. When they could supply goods at international prices and their exports had expanded, new companies were to be given permission to enter the field. However, criticism surfaced many times because of insufficient administrative guidance and uncooperative entrepreneurs.

The First Five-Year Economic Development Plan succeeded thanks to active government involvement. The growth rate of 3.0 percent in the early 1960s became 12.7 percent in 1966, when exports reached US$250 million and foreign currency holdings reached US$240 million. The Economic and Social Modernization of the Republic of Korea, published by the Harvard Institute for International Development and the Korea Development Institute, gave high marks to Korea's achievements. As the book states (p. 464): "In 1961, the First Five-Year Economic and Development Plan (1962–1966) was announced with a target rate of 7 percent per annum. In the light of the economic performance of the early 1960s, this target seemed absurdly high but, in fact, it was exceeded. South Korea, in whose future American advisors had nearly abandoned hope, was on the verge of one of the most rapid sustained growth experiences known to economic history."

The book adds (p. 486): "The strength of the South Korean government is even more obvious in implementation than it is in the formulation of developing policies. In Myrdal's definition, it is indeed a 'hard state' capable of putting its policy measure into effect.

President Park succeeded in raising the Korean economy to the level of other developing country front runners through the Third and Fourth Five-Year Economic Development plans. In 1971 he saved tottering Korean companies facing bankruptcy in the aftermath of Nixon's emergency economic measure by announcing the Emergency Presidential Decree, which froze high interest loans from the informal money market.

President Park promoted and supported enterprises because he deemed them important to economic development, and ultimately to the peaceful reunification of Korea. However, he stressed that entrepreneurs had to feel responsible for the state and the people who had given them a chance. The companies that benefited from the Presidential Emergency Decree vowed that they would repay society by going public. Despite their vows, they did not show much compliance during the next two years, and in May 1974 the president instructed his Cabinet to work for the opening up of enterprises, warning family-owned conglomerates against their incessant expansion efforts via borrowing from the banks. Whenever he heard people mention the word "group," meaning those family-owned conglomerates, he expressed his displeasure, pointing out that some family-owned conglomerates had an unreasonable number of enterprises, concentrating wealth in the hands of a few people and their families, which caused great harm to the sound development of the Korean economy.

Whenever new policies were implemented, the president urged the relevant ministries to take extra care to prevent wealth from becoming even more concentrated in family-owned companies, and to help those companies to become first-rate companies in the field of their specialty in the international market. When he learned about excessive consumption or misbehavior by such owners or their families, he made sure that the issue was addressed because he was concerned that such behavior would harm the unity of the Korean people.